Instructor Books

HANDS-ON SCIENCE

BY SANDRA MARKLE

FUN FACTS AND ACTIVITIES!
Imaginative ideas that lead kids to extend, explore, and discover science throughout the year; Jam-packed with tips for teaching science process skills: observing, classifying, communicating, predicting, and more!!!

FEATURING...
• 12 pull-out task cards • More than 100 reproducibles • Teacher guidelines and suggestions • Ideas to use with the whole class, small groups, individual students, and in your science center • Super Summer Send-Homes • Answer Key

ALL GRADE LEVELS
With special ideas to enhance early learning, K-2

SCHOLASTIC PROFESSIONAL BOOKS

New York • Toronto • London • Auckland • Sydney

SCHOLASTIC INC., 2931 East McCarthy Street, Jefferson City, MO 65102

ISBN 0-590-49035-4

Author, Sandra Markle; Editor, Christine Van Huysse; Illustrator, Joel Rogers; Designers, Eva Shroka, Mark Rook; Copy Editors, Jane Schall, Judy Wechler, and Anne Marie DiTeodoro; Graphics Coordinator, David Komitau; Production Coordinators, Jeanne Johnson, Andrea Junker. The Instructor Books Staff: Ben Miyares, Director; Barbara Michel, Manager.

Contents

Program In Education
CURRICULUM LAB
Bradford College
BRADFORD, MA 01835
(508) 372-7161 X207

Introduction

Throughout the year, Instructor's HANDS-ON SCIENCE will help you teach basic science process skills and excite students about science. Information is presented in a month-by-month format, with a focus on a particular science process skill each month. In September, students learn to make scientific observations. In October, they learn to classify and, in November, to control variables. In the following months, kids build upon these skills and gain experience in making inferences, communicating directions and results, making predictions, and collecting metric measurements. By April, students begin designing experiments. May brings a review of all the process skills. The last chapter lists Super Send-Homes so that students may continue with the process of inquiry begun during the school year.

Each chapter of the book begins with an almanac—a set of science facts based on important or unusual science events—which are cross-referenced to specific activities contained in the chapter. The almanac is followed by a step-by-step presentation of the focus skill. Included each month are ideas for extender activities to enhance student learning, teacher guidelines, and suggestions for using the reproducible pages. These reproducibles are designed to present the activity in an imaginative way and stimulate a sense of inquiry.

Activities are geared to two different levels. One set is developed for students in grades 3 through 8. (More challenging activities are designated by a bubbling flask.) A second set, along with its own reproducibles, is geared for students in kindergarten through second grade. At the very back of the book, you'll find task cards for the most commonly used process skills—observing, classifying, inferring, communicating, predicting, and measuring. Pull these out and place them in a science center or use them as supplementary material for individual students.

Some of the skills and activities covered in HANDS-ON SCIENCE may be too advanced for early primary students. So, each month, a special section is included for children in kindergarten, first, and second grades. A step-by-step introduction presents the process skills in a suitable way. Activities for use with individual students, the whole class, or in science centers provide opportunities for guided practice. Activity pages start beginning readers thinking as they use each skill to solve a problem. After all, at any age, knowing what the appropriate tools are and how to use them to search for a solution are what science is all about.

Kids and science go hand in hand. HANDS-ON SCIENCE will not only strengthen that relationship but encourage students to keep exploring science on their own!

HIGHLIGHTS OF THE MONTH

SEPTEMBER
Focusing on
Observing

3 VIKING II probes Mars' surface in 1976
Ask kids to pretend they're on a space mission making the very first investigations of a planet. Give them the activity "Exploring the Unknown" on pages 12-13, to guide their observations.

4 Kodak box camera patented by George Eastman (U.S.) in 1888
Celebrate this event and provide your students with a chance to observe how light causes changes. Light causing a chemical change on film is what "takes" a picture. Obtain Sunprint paper (see purchasing information, page 10) and give kids the activities "Some Day My Prints Will Come" on page 14 and "Sun Pictures Don't Last" on page 15.

5 First public demonstration of smoke screen given in 1923
Bring a block of dry ice to school in a picnic cooler and take off the lid when you're ready to create a smoke screen. (Check the yellow pages for sources of dry ice.) Does the smoke drift up or down? What happens when someone blows at it? (The smoke sinks because it's colder than the room air and moves when blown, revealing invisible air currents.) Does anybody think this looks like a spooky movie special effect? Good observation—it's often used that way.

10 Elias Howe (U.S.) patents the sewing machine in 1846
Here is a good excuse to bring in cloth samples and let your students observe differences. Can kids find two swatches of the same fabric with their eyes shut?

19 First hot-air balloon with a live crew goes up in 1783
The balloon lifted off from Versailles, France, carrying a rooster, a duck, and a calf. Who invented the hot-air balloon? Have your students do research to find out it was the Montgolfier brothers, Joseph-Michel and Jacques-Étienne. As your class explores hot-air ballooning and flight, you may want to include a creative art activity. Make fanciful model hot-air balloons.

First, color designs on a lunch-sized paper bag. Then, stuff the bag with scrap paper, twist the neck shut and tie it with string. Finish by suspending a small paper cup gondola below the balloon with string. Hang the model balloons from the ceiling.

19 First talking animated film opens in 1928
Can your students guess the identity of the first talking cartoon character? (Mickey Mouse) Ask kids to watch their favorite cartoons, paying attention to how mouth movements match what's said. Give them the activity "Eye Fooled You" on page 16, to observe how animation tricks the eye.

20 George B. Simpson (U.S.) patents the electric range in 1859
A perfect day to plug in an electric griddle! Let kids cook pancakes (use a mix and have students follow the directions on the package). What happens when the batter is first poured on the hot griddle? In what ways does the batter change?

22 The ice cream cone's birthday — 1904
Still hungry? In honor of the cone's birthday, bring in a hand-crank ice cream maker and a churn full of your favorite ice cream ingredients. Challenge your students to explain why rock salt is combined with the ice in the churn. (Salt lowers the melting temperature. As the ice melts, it draws heat from the ice cream mixture.) Time how long it takes to make ice cream and ob-

serve the way the mixture has changed. Then scoop some into cones for a birthday treat!

22 Autumn begins
Even if the trees don't change color where you live, collect some leaves, use a roller to apply some tempera paint to the leaves and make colorful leaf prints. To start kids observing this season, give them the activities "It's a Matter of Tilt" on page 17 and "As the Leaf Turns" on page 18.

23 Neptune first observed in 1846
How was this planet discovered? Both John C. Adams (England) and V. J. Leverrier (France) predicted Neptune's existence and its position through mathematical calculations of what was likely to be true. However, the planet was actually discovered by J. C. Galle—the day after he got Leverrier's prediction. Ask your students to find out what astronomers have observed about Neptune.

25 Centrifugal cream separator patented in 1877
And with cream, you can make butter. Whip some up, following the directions given for "Butter Up!" on page 19. Have intermediate students complete this activity. Then give kids "Moo Mystery" on page 20 to challenge their powers of observation.

26 Johnny Appleseed's birthday — 1774
Pass out apples and the activity "Good to the Core" on page 21, in honor of this American folk hero.

Introducing Observing

Grades 3 and up

Kids grow up exploring the world through their senses—vision, hearing, touch, taste, and smell—and this is the way they continue to investigate anything new. Observing, the skill that requires your students to collect information by using their senses, seems to be the best one to begin with. It is also the process skill scientists use most when they're experimenting.

The biggest difference between the kinds of observations that children are used to making and those that qualify as "scientific" is the attention to detail. Introduce your students to the concept that what they've been doing all their lives—looking, listening, touching, tasting, and smelling—is collecting scientific information. Then help them learn to carefully evaluate this sensory data.

One of the easiest ways to let kids experience using their familiar senses the way a scientist would is to let them observe something change. An inexpensive object that changes quickly, yet is safe enough for young children to handle, is an ice cube. Have enough on hand to give one to each child. Explain to students that it isn't always safe to touch, taste, and smell things. They should never attempt to make observations in this way unless you say it's okay. Next, tell them that in this investigation it's all right to use all of their senses to collect information. Have the children wash their hands. Then distribute the ice cubes in clear plastic cups.

Allow several minutes for silent individual observation. You may want to have a measuring tape and a kitchen scale available for those interested in making more precise observations. Begin to draw out what your students have observed, focusing on one sense at a time. For example, ask how the object looked at the beginning and make a list of the responses on the chalkboard. Let the children know that there are no right or wrong answers. The only rules are to be honest about what is actually observed and to be thorough. Through sharing, help students whose original observations were limited, reevaluate and expand their perceptions.

Explain that observations made using the senses are called *qualitative observations* and that precise measurements made using special instruments are called *quantitative observations*. In a later month, when students are involved in collecting data, they'll focus on measuring.

The ice has probably melted somewhat during the class discussion. Ask your students to observe the ways the object has changed. Have them share their observations, one sense at a time.

EXTENDERS:

September is the beginning of fall. If you live where this season brings colored leaves, colder weather, and birds heading south, there will be many opportunities to observe change. Even if you live where one season is much like another, you can still do the activities given here.

LEAF WATCH
(individual)
SUPPLIES: leaves, paper, pencils
EXPERIENCE: Put a leaf on each child's desk and ask everyone to make brief notes on what the leaf feels, smells, and looks like. Then have the kids record any changes they observe during the next few days. Take time to compare and discuss.

SUGAR-LOVING PLANT
(small groups)
SUPPLIES: warm water (between 110-115° F.), packets of active dry yeast (one tablespoon each), packets of sugar (one teaspoon each), plastic cups
EXPERIENCE: Divide the class into groups. Give each group: ½ cup of water in a plastic cup, 1 packet of yeast, and 3 packets of sugar. Point out what each ingredient is and explain that yeast is a plant but, unlike green plants, it doesn't make its own food. The sugar provides the food the yeast needs to grow—and the changes (expanding bubbling foam) are worth observing. Allow time for students to combine ingredients and to observe and share results.

FOLLOW-UP: Your students may want to do some research to find out in what ways yeast's changes are useful.

USING THE ACTIVITIES:

Pages 12-21 include reproducible activities for students to work on individually or in groups. All stress the process skill of observation and give kids the opportunity to use their senses to explore their environment. Helpful hints for using the activity pages start here. Take a look at each activity before you read the directions for it below. For your convenience, page numbers have been given after each heading in this section.

EXPLORING THE UNKNOWN, pages 12-13
(small groups)
SUPPLIES: test kits made up of an indoor/ outdoor thermometer, a magnifying glass, and a sandwich-size self-sealing plastic bag, a ball of string, timers
EXPERIENCE: Divide your class into groups of up to five students. Distribute one test kit to each group. Then create a test site for each group by spreading a 3-foot-diameter loop of string on the school grounds. Try to place these in different kinds of areas— bare and rocky, grassy, blacktopped, and so forth. Tell the children to investigate the entire site thoroughly, but not to look outside that area. Allow time for the groups to share what they discover. Lead them to the conclusion that a single probe can't provide a complete picture of what a planet is like.

SOME DAY MY PRINTS WILL COME, page 14
(center)
SUPPLIES: a piece of cardboard, an assortment of interestingly-shaped objects to print—a leaf, a key, a piece of lace, and so forth; a timer, a pan of water for rinsing, construction paper, a Sunprint kit and enough extra Sunprint paper for everyone. (Kits, which include Sunprint paper and an acrylic sheet, can be purchased at a moderate price at hobby stores or by mail from Discovery Corner, Lawrence Hall of Science, University of California, Berkeley, CA 94720; 415-642-1016.)
EXPERIENCE: Children can share materials at the science center. Change rinsing water often. Have students mount their finished prints on construction paper and display.
FOLLOW-UP: Encourage your students to do research to find out more about the history of photography, particularly the early Kodak box camera. (It held a roll of film capable of taking 100 round pictures. When the film was ready for processing, the camera was sent off to a laboratory. Later the pictures and reloaded camera were returned—hence the Kodak slogan: You Press the Button, We Do the Rest.)

SUN PICTURES DON'T LAST, page 15
(center)
SUPPLIES: a box or an old bedspread, a flashlight, a small rubber ball, an empty soup can, a birthday candle stuck in a ball of modeling clay
EXPERIENCE: In this activity, your students solve problems by applying what they've learned about being good observers. Set up a dimly-lit area in the science center. Either open a box on one side like a diorama or cover a table with a bedspread and let kids slip into this "darkroom." (On a sunny day take the kids outside and have them observe their shadows.)

EYE FOOLED YOU, page 16
(individual)
SUPPLIES: Have several pieces of movie film available so that students can see a series of photos.
EXPERIENCE: This makes a good activity for kids to take home and do on their own. After your kids have completed their flip-books, create a display so everyone can peek at each others' work. Allow time for your students to share what was difficult about making the book (the hardest part is making only a little change in each picture). Discuss how the flipping speed affects what is seen.
FOLLOW-UP: Encourage your students to research the history of animation or describe how animation has been used in recent movies.

IT'S A MATTER OF TILT, page 17
(whole class & individual)
Encourage your students to check the official times for sunrise and sunset for the first day of fall (usually September 22nd) and figure out how many hours of daylight

10

and how many hours of darkness there are. Explain that this day is called the fall equinox or autumnal equinox because day and night are equal. The earth's tilt affects the position on the horizon of the rising and setting sun and this changes how long the sun appears to take to cross the sky from east to west—the length of a day. Only twice a year, during the spring and fall equinoxes, does the sun rise exactly due east and set exactly due west.
SUPPLIES: five pennies, a flashlight, white paper
EXPERIENCE: Place the supplies in the science center. After your students have had a chance to observe the effect of slanting rays, shine a flashlight at a globe which is held with the North Pole straight up. Repeat this with the North Pole tilted to one side. Your students may be surprised to learn that when it's winter in North America, the Earth is actually closer to the sun. The weather is cold because the northern hemisphere is tilted away from the sun at this time.

AS THE LEAF TURNS, page 18
(whole class)
You may want to go for a walk and let your students collect their own leaves to investigate. Take this activity page along to work outdoors. Kids might also enjoy researching and drawing leaves that are not indigenous to your area. Have children design a game in which pictures of leaves must be matched by type and locale. Have a Leaf Fair with other classes to share discoveries!

BUTTER UP, page 19
(whole class)
SUPPLIES: enough plastic spoons for each student, one pint of whipping cream plus extra cream for samples, water, crackers
EXPERIENCE: Make butter as a class demonstration. First, dip the spoons into the cream and give a spoon to each child to examine. Pour the pint of cream into a blender, whip one minute, and let your students observe. Continue to blend on high until you see thick yellow butter form. Scoop the butter into a bowl and press it with the back of a spoon to force out the remaining milk. Pour on a little fresh water (50° to 70°F). Press the butter again and pour off

the liquid. Repeat until the water is clear. Then give everyone a taste of the butter on a cracker.

MOO MYSTERY, page 20
(center or small groups)
SUPPLIES: milk, whipping cream, two baby food jars with lids or two clear plastic pill bottles with tops, toothpicks
EXPERIENCE: Label one jar *A* and the other *B*. Pour milk into jar A and cream into jar B. (In a science center, supply fresh samples daily.)
FOLLOW-UP: Ask your students to visit a grocery store and list all the different types of fluid milk products they can find. (These will include no fat, skim, 2%, whole, and chocolate. Others may be available in your area.)

GOOD TO THE CORE, page 21
(center)
To launch this activity, share the story of John Chapman, better known as Johnny Appleseed. This folk hero of the early pioneer days is said to have spent nearly 40 years planting apple seeds as he traveled back and forth between the settled farmland in the East and what later became Ohio, Illinois, Indiana, and Iowa. He supposedly collected his apple seeds from cider mills, planted seeds himself, *and* passed out seeds to be planted by others. John Chapman's tombstone is in Fort Wayne, Indiana, and each year, during the third week in September, the Parks and Recreation Department of that city sponsors a festival in his honor.
SUPPLIES: three varieties of apples, six containers with lids, a magnifying glass, a tape measure, a kitchen scale
EXPERIENCE: Label two containers *A*, another two *B*, and the remaining two *C*. Slice some apples of one variety; store the apples and slices separately in the *A* containers. Follow the same procedure for the other varieties, using the *B* and *C* containers. Put fresh slices out each day. To answer the questions, your students will need to use what they've learned about making observations. You may want to suggest words to describe scents, in advance, such as: sweet, fruity, leathery, and so forth, because some kids may find it difficult to describe different smells.

Exploring the unknown

You can imagine how excited scientists were when VIKING II landed on Mars in 1976. They had waited a long time for this chance to actually observe the planet up close. The satellite probe had special instruments to check the air temperature and analyze what gases were in Mars' atmosphere. It was even equipped with a shovel to scoop up soil and an automatic laboratory to test the sample. Basically, the probe was trying to find signs of life by looking for any food or organic wastes. No sign of life, at least not life as we know it, was discovered in Mars' red dirt.

What's it like to probe the unknown? How much can you discover about a planet by exploring one small spot? Find out by pretending you are on a mission to an unexplored planet. Like the crew members of VIKING II, you will be able to investigate only the area immediately around where you land. Take a test kit and go to one of the probe sites which your teacher has prepared. Answer the questions as you explore.

Name _____

1. Is the area you're investigating shaded, partially shaded, or exposed to full sun?

_____

2. Stand and hold the thermometer waist high in front of you. Be sure your fingers don't touch the bulb end of the thermometer. Wait two minutes, then check and record the air temperature. Next, place the thermometer on the ground. Wait another two minutes before you check and record the surface temperature.

Air Temperature _____   Surface Temperature _____

3. Looking down on it, observe your probe area. Describe what you see. _____

_____

_____

_____

4. Touch the surface. Examine it with the magnifying glass. What do you feel and see?

_____

_____

Put a small sample of the surface material into a self-sealing plastic bag and attach it to this page.

5. Do you see any living organisms or any evidence that living organisms have once been in this area (for example, tracks, dead bodies or body parts, dried leaves or feathers). If so, describe what you discovered on the back of this page.

Name _____

Some day my prints will come

Photography started with the observation that silver salts turn dark when exposed to light and that chemicals can be used to make this change permanent. But it wasn't until George Eastman invented the Kodak box camera in 1888 that taking pictures became inexpensive and easy enough for amateurs.

Try this experiment to see how sunlight causes a chemical change to produce a picture and answer the questions about your observations. Choose some items to print from among those your teacher has provided. Take the objects you chose, a Sunprint kit, cardboard, and a timer outside or close to a sunny window. After you've laid down the cardboard, take one sheet of Sunprint paper out of the black plastic bag and put the paper on the cardboard, blue side up. Quickly arrange the items you're printing. If they're flat, cover them with the plastic sheet. Set the timer for five minutes.

1. What change do you observe as the Sunprint paper is exposed to the light?

_____

_____

_____

2. Rinse the Sunprint paper in a pan of water for about a minute. What happens as you rinse?

_____

_____

_____

3. Lay the paper on a dry, flat surface. How does the print change as the paper dries?

_____

_____

_____

Name _____

14

Sun pictures don't last

The sun makes pictures every time it shines. Those pictures are shadows and they're everywhere. Just look around you. While the sun's pictures don't last, they're both interesting and helpful. Shadows make it easier to tell an object's shape and they show if something is rough or smooth. Go outside and observe your shadow. What do you see?

_____

_____

Take a ball, a soup can, and a clay ball with a birthday candle stuck into it. Shine a flashlight at each object to see what its shadow looks like. Then match the pictures below by drawing a line from each object to its shadow.

Objects can also have many different shadows. Direct the flashlight's beam at the ball in each of the ways shown in the diagrams. Which way makes the longest shadow? Circle the correct diagram. How many other shadows are you able to create by changing the way you hold the flashlight?

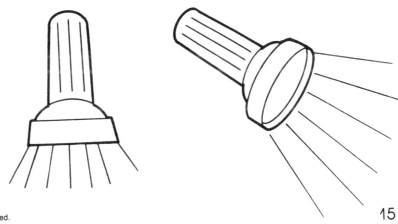

Name _____

Eye fooled you

One familiar example of an optical illusion is a motion picture. If you look at a piece of movie film, you will see that it is actually a series of single photos, each varying slightly from the ones before and after it. When this set of photos is projected for you at the right speed, the images seem to run together. This occurs because of "persistence of vision." An image that appears on the retina of your eye is retained there for a fraction of a second and a *series* of images then blend together to give the impression of motion. The film technique called animation takes advantage of this persistence of vision, too. But in a cartoon, the frames are often made up of drawings. Try this investigation to prove that moving pictures are really only an optical illusion.

Materials: Four sheets of paper, scissors, a stapler, markers

1. Fold the sheets of paper in half. Unfold the paper and cut on the crease. Stack the half-sheets, fold them, and cut along the new crease. You should have 16 small pages. Match the papers evenly along the uncut edge and staple on one side to form a book.

2. On the first page, draw an image of a person, animal, or thing. On the second page, draw the same image, but change it slightly. Repeat your picture on the third page and change it a little more. Keep making these drawings, changing each one slightly, until you reach the back of your book. For example, on the first page, you might draw a stick figure with its arms down. On the second page, the figure could have one arm raised just a little, and on the third page, the arm could be raised a little higher. Continue drawing the figure. By the middle of the book, the arm might be raised above the head. By the end, it should have come all the way back down.

3. Watch the pictures as you flip through the book slowly. Watch again as you flip through quickly. Describe how speeding up changes how the image appears to move.

_____

_____

Name _____

It's a matter of tilt

Complete orbit is 365 ¼ days

Fall officially starts on September 22nd. Have you noticed that the sun's rays no longer seem as hot as they did during the summer? A noontime shadow during the summer is very short. What does your shadow look like at noontime now? These changes are caused by the fact that Earth is tilted as it orbits the sun. Try this investigation to observe how the angle at which light rays strike an object makes a difference in its shadow.

Hold a flashlight about six inches above a piece of white paper. Stack five pennies on the paper and shine the light straight down on the stack. Observe carefully. Describe everything you see.

_____

_____

Repeat this test, holding the flashlight at an angle. Describe how the slanting rays change what you see.

_____

_____

Name _____

As the leaf turns

Trees that shed their leaves get ready for winter by producing a separation layer at the base of each leaf. At the same time, the leaf stops producing chlorophyll, the green chemical needed to manufacture sugar. As the chlorophyll breaks down, the other colored pigments in the leaf become visible. Are color and structure the only ways that fall leaves differ from green summer leaves?

Compare a brightly colored leaf to a green leaf. Use all your senses except taste to find out how the two leaves are different. Tell what you observed.

_____

_____

_____

_____

Find a leaf that has fallen off. Poke the end of the stem with your fingernail. Describe what you feel. _____

_____

_____

Now look at a twig. You'll see leaf scars where the leaves used to be attached. Examine one with a magnifying glass. The spots on these scars are the ends of the tubes through which water traveled up to the leaf from the roots and sugar moved down to be stored. Draw a picture of a leaf scar.

Name _____

18

Butter up!

Cows don't give butter. Did you ever wonder how butter is made? Watch the demonstration and write down your observations.

1. First examine the cream. What senses can you use to collect information?

   _____

   What did you observe? _____

   _____

2. How has the whipping cream changed after one minute?

   _____

3. Then use your senses to examine the finished butter. Describe your observations.

   _____

   _____

4. Look at your original and final observations. In what ways did the cream change when it became butter?

   _____

   _____

5. On the back make a list of all the foods you like to eat with butter on them.

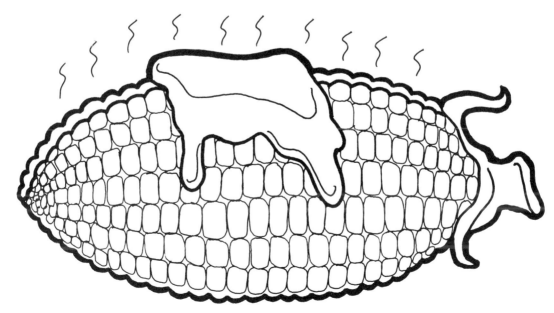

Name _____

Moo mystery

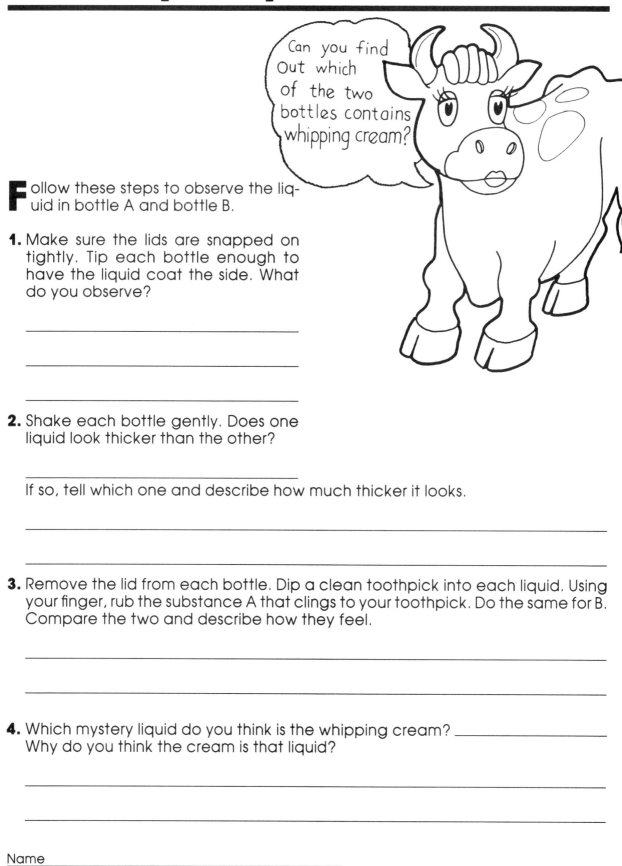

Can you find Out which of the two bottles contains whipping cream?

Follow these steps to observe the liquid in bottle A and bottle B.

1. Make sure the lids are snapped on tightly. Tip each bottle enough to have the liquid coat the side. What do you observe?

_____

_____

_____

2. Shake each bottle gently. Does one liquid look thicker than the other?

_____

If so, tell which one and describe how much thicker it looks.

_____

_____

3. Remove the lid from each bottle. Dip a clean toothpick into each liquid. Using your finger, rub the substance A that clings to your toothpick. Do the same for B. Compare the two and describe how they feel.

_____

_____

4. Which mystery liquid do you think is the whipping cream? _____
Why do you think the cream is that liquid?

_____

_____

Name _____

Good to the core

There are more than 6,500 varieties of apples in the world (about 1,000 varieties are grown in the United States). How different are apples? You'll need a whole apple and a slice of each of the samples—A, B, and C—supplied by your teacher.

1. In what ways do the apples look different? (You may want to use a tape measure or magnifying glass.)

_____

_____

_____

_____

_____

2. Do they smell different? Is one sweeter smelling? Does one have a stronger scent? Describe what you smell.

_____

_____

_____

_____

3. Take a bite of each apple slice. Describe how each slice tastes. Which is the sweetest? Do the apples feel different in your mouth? Tell in what way.

_____

_____

4. What is another observation you can make to compare the three apple varieties?

_____

_____

_____

Name _____

Especially for K—2
Introducing Observing

Young children readily accept their senses—seeing, hearing, touching, tasting, and smelling—as useful exploratory tools, but they need to expand their powers of observation. If you live where the leaves turn beautiful colors, bring fall into your classroom. Fill a child's wading pool or a big box with colorful leaves. Have everyone gather around the leaf pile. Tasting is out but let each child grab a handful to sniff. Talk about the smell of fall leaves. You may want to have some fresh green leaves available for your students to compare the aromas. Next have students rub several leaves together or crumple some in their hands. Have students describe the texture of the leaves or the sounds made when leaves are crumpled. The children can also compare the sound and the touch of colored leaves to green leaves.

Finally, help your students to expand the use of their most familiar sense, sight. Ask them to describe how one leaf differs from another. Is one scalloped, long, brick-colored? Tell them to search for and hold up the prettiest leaf they can find in the pile.

If you don't live where leaves change in the fall, try a similar sensory experience by having children explore an assortment of cloth scraps. Then expand either introductory experience by helping your students observe signs of the season. Keep a sky calendar to record whether the weather is sunny or cloudy. (Each day, let the children color a bright sun or glue on a cottonball cloud.) Go for a walk to collect nature debris—bark, bird feathers, nutshells, and fallen leaves. If you're lucky enough to find a caterpillar, put it in a jar that has holes punched in the lid. Place leaves and branches in the jar for food. The caterpillar may spin a cocoon while your students watch. Keep the cocoon in a cool place so that the butterfly or moth won't appear before spring, then you can set it free.

You can also hold a sensory memory hunt. Gather your students into a big circle. Tell them to sit still and picture something in their minds that is yellow. Ask several different children for answers. Then, ask them to think of something that fits each of these descriptions: soft, scratchy, blue, warm, noisy, smells good, slippery, and red.

EXTENDERS:
I'M SPECIAL
(center)
SUPPLIES: paper, staples, a self-supporting mirror, a tape measure
EXPERIENCE: This activity encourages students to observe themselves more closely and to realize that they are unique and, therefore, special. Prepare a four-page booklet for each child. First, design fill-in-the-blank worksheets for the last three pages:
Page 2, "All about Me"—Include questions about all the personal data you want kids to observe about themselves, such as hair color, eye color, and height.
Page 3, "My Favorite Things"—List a favorite food, flavor of ice cream, toy, activity, friend's name, and so forth. Also include a space for the child to draw a picture of a favorite toy or pet.
Page 4, "My Family"—Provide space for children to draw a family portrait and a place to list the names and ages of brothers and sisters. You might give them an opportunity to describe a favorite family activity, as well.

Copy the worksheets. Make up the booklets by putting the pages in order (page 1 should be blank). Staple along the left side. Glue a snapshot of each child on the "cover" of his or her booklet, or have each child draw a self-portrait on the cover.

Before starting the activity, arrange with teachers of older students to loan helpers who can assist you with nonreaders. (If the older kids are not expert readers, participating in this way gives them a chance to be successful.)

MYSTERY SOUNDS
(whole class)
SUPPLIES: audio cassette tape, tape recorder
EXPERIENCE: This activity is designed to encourage students to observe the world using their sense of hearing. Tape familiar sounds, such as a telephone ringing, water

running, and a door opening. Sit with the children in a circle. Play each sound one by one and ask, "What makes this sound?" If the first guess is incorrect, tell your students to think about where they have heard the sound. Play the taped sound again. If the next guess is also incorrect, tell the answer and play the sound again as reinforcement. If your students miss a number of the sounds, repeat this game at a later time. If they do well, play again, using a new set of sounds.

USING THE ACTIVITIES:

The reproducible activities on pages 24-26 give kids a chance to sharpen their ability to use the process skill observation. Look at each activity (see the page numbers following) before you read the comments about it on this page.

ANIMAL TALES, page 24
(individual)
This activity provides young children with an opportunity to call on memories of observations and use these to solve problems.

ALL IN THE FAMILY, page 25
(small group)
Do this activity with a group of four or five children while the other students are involved at learning centers. Guide kids through looking for the items in each set and deciding what these have in common. Then help students decide why the one item is different. Each group may want to make up sets for other groups to solve and discuss.

Animal tales

Something about each of these animals is wrong. Find what does not belong and draw a circle around it.

Oops! Each of these animals is making the wrong sound. Draw a line to connect each animal to the sound it really makes.

Name _____

All in the family

Draw a circle around the one thing that does not belong in each set.

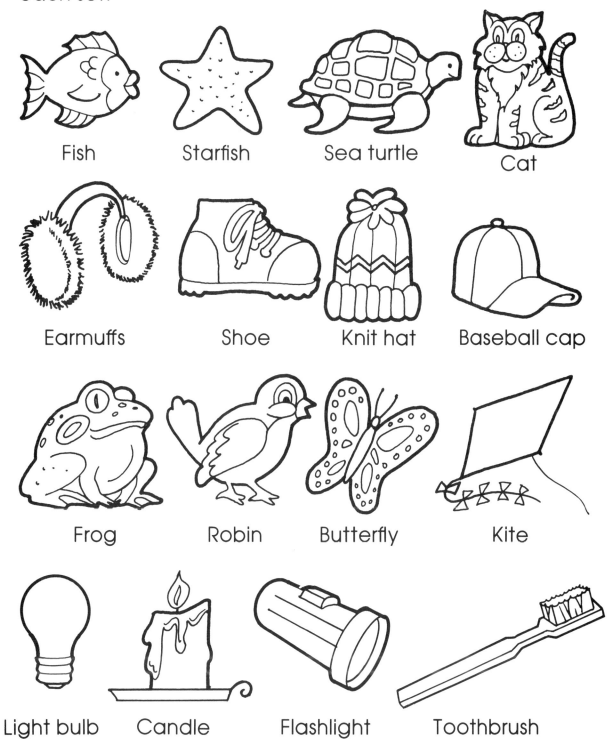

Fish   Starfish   Sea turtle   Cat

Earmuffs   Shoe   Knit hat   Baseball cap

Frog   Robin   Butterfly   Kite

Light bulb   Candle   Flashlight   Toothbrush

Name

Copy cat

One of these cats has a twin. Draw a line to connect the pair.

Name _____

HIGHLIGHTS OF THE MONTH

OCTOBER
Focusing on
Classifying

4 Russians Launch SPUTNIK I in 1957

The orbiting of this man-made Earth satellite whose name means "fellow traveler of Earth," was heralded as the beginning of the Space Age. To celebrate the event that marked man's first exploration beyond Earth, turn to the activity "Satellite Sort" on pages 32-33.

4 Russia's Luna 3 transmits the first pictures of the far side of the moon — 1959.

Take time tonight to look at the moon. Give your students the activity "Crater Capers" on pages 34-35.

5 Robert Goddard (U.S.) born in 1882

Discover facts about rockets and hold a launch of your own in honor of the "father of modern rocketry." For help with these activities, turn to "3, 2, 1, Blast Off!" on pages 36-37.

9 Beginning of Fire Prevention Week

Celebrated annually since 1925, this week commemorates the great Chicago fire of 1871. How did this fire start? Have your students research to find out. (Mrs. O'Leary's cow knocked over a lantern.) Ask your students to check for overloaded outlets, frayed cords on appliances, lamps that have bulbs with too high wattage, or improperly stored flammable household products. Have kids classify what they find into two groups: fire-safe items and fire hazards. Arrange for a firefighter to visit and talk about what to do in case of fire.

10 First synthetic detergent for home use marketed by Procter & Gamble in 1933

Let your students work in small groups to test how well each of five brands of detergent cleans ketchup and mud-stained fabric squares. To test each brand, have kids half fill a clear plastic pill bottle with water, add one-half teaspoon of detergent, and push in a stained cloth. Then have them cap the bot-

tle and shake vigorously for one minute to simulate washing machine action. After the tests, ask your students to group the detergents into two groups: those that removed the stains and those that didn't.

14 Charles E. Yeager made the first faster-than-the-speed-of sound flight in 1947
Ask your students to find out more about the attributes of supersonic aircraft.

21 Thomas A. Edison invented the first practical incandescent electric lamp in 1879
Switch on the lights and give your students the activity "You Light Up My Life" on pages 38-39.

23 Nicolas Appert (France) born in 1752
Open a can in honor of the man known as the "father of canning." Then, to start kids thinking about the attributes of canned food, turn to pages 40-41 for "In The Can."

28 Jonas Salk (U.S.) born in 1914
In honor of the man who developed a vaccine for polio, devote time to classifying common diseases such as measles and mumps according to whether or not a vaccine exists for them.

30 John J. Loud (U.S.) patented the ballpoint pen in 1888
Ask kids to think of categories that could be used to classify ballpoint pens (colors of ink, erasable ink, ability to write upside down, replaceable ink cartridge, etc). Encourage doodling while thinking, with a ballpoint pen, of course!

Week beginning the second Sunday is National School Lunch Week
Ask kids to keep track of what they eat and then classify these foods into the four basic food groups: 1. breads and cereals; 2. fruits and vegetables; 3. milk and other dairy products; and 4. meat, eggs, nuts, and beans. To be healthy and feel good, kids need four servings daily from group 1 & 2, three from group 3, and two from group 4. Which group is the favorite among your students? The least? Do they need to eat more of certain foods?

Week beginning the third Sunday is National Forest Products Week
October is the month when trees reach their peak color in many areas. Encourage kids to take time to look at trees. The activities "It's Unbe-leaf-able!" on page 42, and "Name That Leaf" on page 43, will help your students understand how to use classifying to identify different kinds of tree leaves.

All month: National Popcorn Poppin' Month
What a great excuse to pop and munch—all in the interest of comparing different brands of popcorn! Ask your students to observe such attributes as the total number of kernels that popped in a batch, the average kernel size, and the taste. Have fun classifying!

All month: Spectacle of the Geese
Geese, other birds, and a number of animals are migrating this month. Ask your students to watch for traveling birds. Help kids use classifying to find out more about migratory animals. Give them the activity "Animals on the Move" on page 44.

Introducing Classifying
Grades 3 and up

Like observing, classifying is a basic process skill children use naturally, although not necessarily with scientific precision. Anytime they sort things into groups or make a choice based on differences they've observed, kids are classifying. To introduce this skill, help your students recognize that many familiar everyday choices are done by classifying. For example, selecting healthy food instead of spoiled is classifying. So is choosing clothes to wear that look good together.

Explain to your students that what they're really doing is observing some particular property, like mold or color, and using that to separate objects into groups. Tell them that scientists call such properties *attributes*, and that classification is also used to sort people and events. To illustrate, call all the children with blonde hair by name and ask them to stand together in one group, apart from the others. Point out that you've just classified the students into two groups and ask who can tell the attribute you used to do it. You may want to expand this introductory experience, sorting the children by different attributes, such as boys and girls, or those wearing blue and those not, and challenge your students to identify what attribute you used each time.

Up until now, your students have been doing a kind of instinctive classifying—in most cases not even thinking about what they're observing to make sorting choices. To be able to use this skill the way a scientist does, students need to learn to look for attributes and thoughtfully use those traits to create groups. Scientists often work with what is called a *key*, which allows them to make a series of classification choices to identify something specific, such as a type of bird or a kind of rock. In one of this month's activities, your students will learn to use a scientific key to identify specific kinds of leaves.

To teach kids to classify the way a scientist does, use the jack-o-lantern attribute card, page 48. First, divide your class into small groups. Then, run off enough copies to give one set to each group. Ask someone in the group to cut them apart. Challenge the groups to look for attributes

that make one jack-o-lantern different from another and to find as many of these as possible. Allow time to work and then let the groups share their choices as you write a list on the chalkboard. This exchange of ideas encourages students to be thorough and to expand their viewpoints.

Next, write the attribute "has a hat" on the board (or circle this attribute if it's on the list). Tell your students that you want them to classify their jack-o-lanterns into two groups—those that have the attribute and those that don't. When they've accomplished this, challenge them to use three more attributes to sort the jack-o-lanterns. Again, allow time to work and share.

Now, ask your students to pull out the cards showing the jack-o-lantern with the baseball cap. Tell them to place this card on a desk top and then to find another card with a jack-o-lantern that differs by only one attribute. Have them line up two or more cards so that each one differs by only one attribute from the card preceding it. Several correct answers are possible here, so you'll probably want to circulate to check the results. Repeat this activity, challenging your students to see how many jack-o-lanterns they can line up that are different from the preceding one by two attributes.

EXTENDERS:

WHAT SHAPE ARE YOUR LEAVES IN?
(whole class)
SUPPLIES: a variety of leaves of different shapes
EXPERIENCE: Give your students more practice in identifying attributes and classifying with this leaf-sorting activity. Bring in the leaves yourself or have the class go on a walk and collect them. In the classroom, ask kids to look for such attributes as serrated edges and leaflets and use these shape characteristics to put the leaves into categories. You may also want to have students sort the leaves by color.

USING THE ACTIVITIES:

The reproducible activities on pages 32-44 allow students to practice finding attributes and classifying. Teacher notes and page numbers for each activity are given below. Be sure to look at the activity before you read the comments here.

SATELLITE SORT, pages 32-33
(individual)
Give your students this activity to provide them with more practice in looking for attributes and classifying and to introduce them to satellite use and equipment. After kids research their chosen satellites, review the structure and function of satellites with them. Then help them incorporate what they've learned about the attributes of satellites to design one themselves. You might also want to have kids use their designs to make three-dimensional models. Display the models around the classroom.

CRATER CAPERS, pages 34-35
(center)
SUPPLIES: plaster of Paris, water, salt, empty half-pint milk cartons, marbles, spoons, rulers
EXPERIENCE: What are moon craters like? Have kids do this activity to find out as they examine close-up pictures of real moon craters, looking for attributes. Reinforce last month's skill by reviewing observation and encourage kids to observe carefully as they create their own craters.

3, 2, 1 BLAST OFF!, pages 36-37
(small group)
SUPPLIES: a spool of monofilament fishing line, masking tape, plastic straws cut in half, enough balloons to give one to each child, enough tape measures to give one to each group
EXPERIENCE: Before you have the class do this activity, think of some ways to keep pieces of the fishing line stretched taut, across your classroom. To create launch teams, divide the class into small groups. Let group members work through classifying the rockets together. Then distribute the launch lines—one to a group to save time.

Next, have the class follow the directions in "Hold Your Own Launch," and explain how to set up the lines. Ask each group to use the tape measure to determine how far the rockets travel on the line. Encourage the children to measure carefully. Have each group report on its farthest flight. Graph the results of the class. Older children might figure out a group average and explain differences in the results.

YOU LIGHT UP MY LIFE, pages 38-39
(individual)
Help your students learn about the electric bulb, a household staple, with this simple take-home activity that provides good practice in identifying attributes and classifying. Kids won't need much help doing "You Light Up My Life." However, you might want to demonstrate how different wattages affect bulb brightness by testing a selection of bulbs on lamps in the classroom.

IN THE CAN, pages 40-41
(small groups)
SUPPLIES: cans of regular and "lite" foods
EXPERIENCE: Before you have students do this activity, help them understand the importance of reading food-can labels. Discuss how using canned food that is low in salt and sugar can lead to better health. Pass around the sample food cans so kids can examine them.
FOLLOW-UP: Take a class of younger children on a guided tour of a supermarket so they can read food-can labels and see how the store groups foods in sections. Have older children go "shopping" on their own after school hours. First, make up five different shopping lists of items commonly found on supermarket shelves. Then divide the class into five groups and give everyone in group 1 a copy of list 1, everyone in group 2 a copy of list 2, and so forth. Have kids search through a supermarket to find particular sections for items on the lists. Let them try their hand at seeing how their classification skills match up to the supermarket's. After students turn in this homework, ask the groups to switch lists and repeat the exercise.

IT'S UNBE-LEAF-ABLE!, page 42
(individual and whole class)
Have your students complete this activity at home. Allow time for each child to share a favorite leaf in class and tell what attribute he or she likes about it. You may also want to display the leaves that kids press and mount.

NAME THAT LEAF, page 43*
(individual)
With this activity, you challenge your students to apply what they've learned about identifying attributes and sorting objects. After the kids have used the activity's key to name the pictured leaves, encourage them to try making their own keys for leaves they've found. It isn't necessary for their keys to lead them to a leaf's official name. Kids can make leaf keys that help them find leaf A, B, C, and so on. Being able to generate their own scientific keys shows that they really understand how to classify. For further practice in using keys, you might want to have the kids exchange and test each other's keys.

ANIMALS ON THE MOVE, page 44*
(individual and whole class)
Encourage your students to think and analyze the facts carefully as they search for attributes used to classify migratory animals. Allow time for the kids to discuss what attributes they picked and why they made those choices. After students research the selected animals, create a science center lending library with their reports. Or provide time in class for them to share their findings.

*Challenging activity

Satellite sort

E ver wonder what satellites look like and what job they do? Here are pictures and facts.

1. ECHO II: This early communications satellite was a giant balloon, nearly 135 feet in diameter. Radio signals were bounced off its surface.

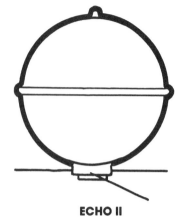

ECHO II

2. TIROS: The surface was covered with solar cells for power. It had two television cameras which scanned Earth's atmosphere sending back weather pictures.

TIROS

5. NIMBUS: This solar-powered satellite sent back data about Earth's upper atmosphere as well as weather information.

NIMBUS

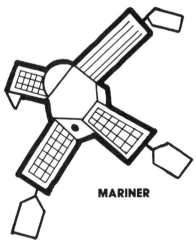

MARINER

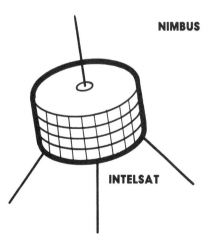

INTELSAT

4. INTELSAT: This solar-powered satellite, only 28 inches in diameter, could relay 240 two-way telephone conversations at one time.

3. MARINER: This long distance traveler was powered by solar cells on its big paddle arms. Its cameras took the first close-up pictures of Mars.

Name _____

Now that you've read the descriptions of satellites on page 32, you're ready to group these satellites by **attributes,** or qualities. First, look at the example in the chart below to see how the attribute "cameras" was used to sort the satellites. To complete the chart, classify the satellites by two other attributes. For each one, name the attribute in the first column, then show the satellites that **have it** in the second column and those that **don't have it** in the third column. Be sure that you can find each attribute in more than one satellite.

	Attribute	Have It	Don't Have It
1.	Cameras	Tiros, Mariner	Echo II, Nimbus, Intelsat
2.			
3.			

Several other famous satellites are listed below on the left. Choose one to explore and circle it. Use books and encyclopedias to help you answer the fact-list questions on the right. Then use what you discovered to add this satellite to the chart.

Viking   What was its job? _____

Pioneer   _____

Voyager II   How was it powered? _____

Solar Max   Did it have any cameras? _____

Telstar I   What other special features did it have? _____

                _____

Now pretend your job is to design a satellite. Draw a picture of your satellite on a piece of paper and make a fact list to describe it's attributes.

Name _____

Crater capers

While the earth has only a few craters, or holes in its surface, the moon has many of them. Using close-up satellite views, scientists have been able to identify a number of attributes that they can use to classify the moon's craters. Examine these pictures of moon craters. The example given tells one feature of the craters. List three more features you think might make good attributes for classifying craters.

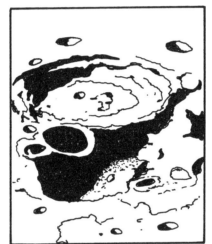
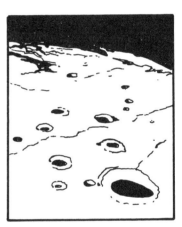

Crater Attributes

1. Mountains in the center

2.

3.

4.

Name

Meteorites are believed to have caused most of the moon's craters. To find out how this happened, cut the top off an empty half-pint milk container. Fill it half full of plaster of Paris powder and stir in enough water to make the plaster as thick as pancake batter. Mix in a half teaspoon of salt to make the plaster harden more quickly. When the surface is almost firm, drop a marble from about two inches above the plaster. Carefully pick out the marble and look at the plaster. What do you see? Next drop the marble from about four inches.

1. Based on this experiment, what do you suppose a meteorite is?

_____

2. Describe what the first crater you made looks like.

_____

3. Since the marble dropped farther the second time, it hit the surface harder. How is this crater different from the first?

_____

4. Some of the moon's craters have rays spreading out from them. Based on your observations, what do you think may have caused these rays?

_____

_____

Name _____

3, 2, 1, Blast off!

Robert Goddard invented the first successful liquid-fuel rocket. Like today's rock giants, it had a liquid-oxygen tank and a smaller gasoline tank in its tail. These fuel tanks were connected by tubes to a **combustion chamber** in its nose. The fuel was burned there to produce flaming gases. For his pioneer efforts, Robert Goddard is often called "the father of modern rocketry."

Use the pictures and facts below to compare these U.S. rockets.

   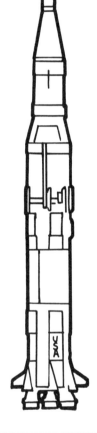

Rocket	Scout	Atlas-Agena	Delta	Saturn V*
Weight	72 ft.	102 ft.	116 ft.	363 ft.
Number of stages	4	2	3	3
Type of fuel	solid	liquid	Stages 1 & 2: liquid Stage 3: solid	Liquid

*This rocket carried astronauts to the moon.

Name _____

Look at the example. Then find two more attributes and use them to sort the rockets.

Attribute	Have It	Don't Have It
1. Solid fuel	Scout, Delta	Atlas-Agena, Saturn V
2.		
3.		

Hold Your Own Launch

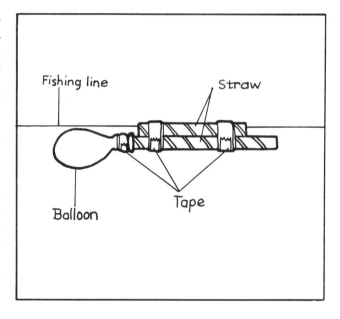

You don't need special fuel to explore rocket propulsion. Try this experiment to find out what makes a rocket move. Take two straws. Cut one straw 1 ¼ inches shorter than the other. Tape a balloon to the end of the long straw. Then tape the short straw to the long one, as shown in the diagram. Thread a long piece of fishing line through the short straw. Anchor the fishing line to opposite sides of the room. (Your teacher will give you specific directions.) Next pull the straw to the end of the line. Blow up the balloon and pinch the neck shut. Release the neck of the balloon and watch it travel along the fishing line!

1. Gases surging from a rocket engine's nozzles propel the rocket away from the earth. Air rushing out of your balloon's neck is just like the hot gases in a rocket. How far did your balloon travel before it stopped?

_____

2. How could you make your balloon-rocket go even farther?

_____

Name _____

You light up my life

Today there are a wide variety of light bulbs to choose from. Bulbs differ in their color, shape, and in the amount of watts they use. A **watt** is a measurement of electric power. The more watts a bulb uses, the brighter it is. Look at the selection of bulbs shown below. Then complete the chart to classify them.

Candlelight Bulb

25 watt

clear

flame tipped

Colored Party Bulb

40 watt

clear red

round

Floodlight

250 watt

frosted white

cone shaped

Appliance Bulb

40 watt

clear

round

Standard Bulb

150 watt

frosted white

teardrop shaped

Name _____

38

Bulb Sort		
Attribute	Have It	Don't Have It
1.		
2.		
3.		

At the bottom of this page list all the different kinds of bulbs you can find in use around your house. (Do not touch any bulbs.) If you have trouble identifying a bulb, ask an adult to help you.

Name _____

In the can

You've probably never heard of Nicolas Appert, but you eat better because of his invention. Appert developed a system of heating foods and sealing them in air-tight containers. Before his invention, people ate fruits, vegetables, and many other foods, only in season.

Use these labels to classify the three brands of chicken soup. Remember ingredients are listed in descending order: the soup contains the most of the first item and the least of the last item.

SO FINE
Use before December 1989
Ingredients: chicken, water, salt, sugar, chicken stock, vegetables
189 calories per 1/2 cup serving

CHEF'S CHOICE
Use before December 1989
Ingredients: chicken, chicken stock, mixed vegetables, water
200 calories per 1/2 cup serving

YUMMY SOUP
Best if used before
January 1992
Ingredients: water, chicken stock, salt, assorted vegetables, chicken parts
110 calories per 1/2 cup serving

1. Which brands contain more chicken than any other ingredient?

_____

2. Which brands have salt added?

_____

3. Which brands have sugar added?

_____

4. What is another attribute that you can use to sort these canned soups?

_____

Name _____

How do canned foods add to your family's diet? Look in your pantry at home. What kinds of canned food are there in each of the categories? List this number on the chart.

Meats	Fruits	Vegetables

Juices	Soups	Snacks

1. What is your favorite canned food?

_____

2. How much of your family's evening dinner comes from a can?

_____

3. List all the canned foods that are included in your meal

_____

_____

Use taste to classify foods. List at least five foods that you like canned and five that you prefer fresh or frozen.

Taste Good Canned   **Better Fresh or Frozen**

1.   1.

2.   2.

3.   3.

4.   4.

5.   5.

Name _____

It's unbe-leaf-able

Materials: leaves, newspaper, books, construction paper, clear contact paper (optional)

Directions: This is a good time to take a closer look at trees. Collect at least five different leaves. Preserve them by placing them between layers of newspaper. Stack books on top to press the leaves flat. After a week, tape each dried leaf to construction paper or press them between two sheets of contact paper. Now, you're ready to classify the leaves you collected. Study the attributes pointed out below. Search for these attributes in your leaves. Examine the edges, the tips, and the surface lines (called veins). Use these attributes, or others, to sort your leaves.

Pointed Tip

Lobed Edges

Serrated Edges

Alternating Veins

List two other attributes that can be used to sort your leaves.

_____

_____

Name _____

42

Name that leaf

When scientists have to identify different things like leaves, they use a tool called a key. Here is a key to help you name the mystery leaves. To use it, start with leaf number 1. Then decide which of the attributes--needles or broad leaf--fits this leaf. Next, look at the number to the right of the attribute you chose. This number tells you which step in the key to advance to. For example, if you picked broad leaf, go to step 3 and choose between the two attributes listed there. Keep making choices and advancing until you find a name next to the attribute. This identifies the leaf so write that name next to the picture. Then work on identifying leaf number 2.

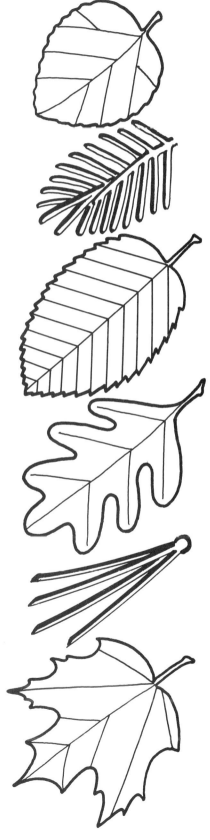

I. Needles 2
    Broad leaves 3

2. Needles in clusters . . . . Pine
    Needles all over the
    branches . . . . Spruce

3. Lobed 4
    Not Lobed 5

4. Sharp lobes . . . . Maple
    Rounded Lobes . . . . Oak

5. Sharp teeth . . . . Elm
    Rounded teeth . . . . Poplar

Name _____

Animals on the move

All the animals named on this page migrate—or move from one area to another—during certain times each year. Read over the facts given about the animals. Use the information to classify the animals on the chart below.

BATS:
migrate at night, fly in groups of 100 or more, usually go 20-50 miles

ALASKA FUR SEALS:
males and females travel in separate groups, migrate thousands of miles

MONARCH BUTTERFLIES:
large flocks travel by day, may cover as much as 1,500 miles; they fly low, about 15 feet above the ground

CARIBOU:
travel in large herds; walk by day; travel a total of 500-600 miles

PENGUINS:
males and females travel in separate groups; swim nearly 500 miles and then walk inland another few hundred miles during the Antarctic summer

Mystery Attribute

Attribute	Have It	Don't Have It
	Bats, Monarchs	Caribou, Seals, Penguins,
	Seals, Penguins	Bats, Caribou, Monarchs

Choose one of the animals listed above and use books and encyclopedias to find out more about its life, particularly why it travels and where it goes. Write your report on a separate sheet of paper. You may want to include a picture.

Name _____

Especially for K—2
Introducing Classifying

Explain to kids that in order for scientists to conduct experiments, they need to classify—how things, people, and events are alike and how they are different. For a fun introductory sorting experience, cut five giant pumpkin shapes out of orange poster board. In each pumpkin, cut two holes that are big enough to slip a child's arm through. Space the holes so that when a child puts on a poster pumpkin the top will be just below his or her chin. Next, turn each pumpkin into a jack-o-lantern by painting on a face and adding extras, such as ears. Select five students to put on these jack-o-lantern costumes.

When these pumpkin people are lined up before the class, ask your students to tell you every way that the pumpkins are alike (big, round, orange, have faces). Then ask them to think of one way that the pumpkins differ. (For example, some are smiling and some are not.) Pick out one person with a smiling pumpkin and call on all other smiling pumpkins to gather around. Form the other pumpkin people into a separate group. To make this sorting into two groups even clearer, mark off two circles on the floor with tape. When your students name a different attribute to re-sort the groups, point out that it's possible to classify the same things in a number of different ways.

To continue developing this skill, go for a leaf-collecting walk. Ask your students to find three leaves that are alike in some way. At first, you may want to provide more guidance by telling them to look for leaves that are the same color, shape, or size. Next, have them find someone else who has leaves that are like theirs. Challenge each pair to also find leaves that differ. Take time to sit down in a circle and let each pair describe how their leaves are alike and different.

Or, play animal sort. This is a good game to play outside or in the gym. Tell your students to pretend to be either a frog, a bird, a cat, or a snake. Have them make appropriate sounds or move like the animal of their choice. When you say go, challenge your students to find all the others of their kind and group themselves.

EXTENDERS:
TOUCH AND SORT
(center)
Choose objects that have attributes that can be felt. Examples are wooden items, sponges, rocks, and so on. Put each item into the toe of a tube sock and mark the sock with a number. Then instruct your students to sort these items into groups by the way the items feel. Remind the children that size doesn't count.

PUMPKIN BAGS
(whole class)
Many cities celebrate this harvest season with pumpkin festivals. Jack-o-lanterns are another popular Halloween tradition. Here's an activity that is both a seasonal art project and an exercise to develop classifying skills.
SUPPLIES: one lunch-size paper bag for each child, newspaper, rubber bands, tempera paints, marking pens, colored papers, construction paper, scraps of yarn, felt, fabric, ribbon, glitter, beads
EXPERIENCE: Have your students make their own pumpkins by stuffing a lunch sack with wads of newspaper. Twist the neck to create a stem. Secure it in several places with rubber bands. Next, have them paint their pumpkins. When the paint is dry, a face may be added with markers or by cutting pieces of construction paper. The pumpkins might also be decorated with ribbon, lace, felt, or other materials.

When you're ready to practice classifying, mark off two big circles on the floor with tape. Let your students suggest an attribute that can be used to sort the bag pumpkins. Then tell all the students who have pumpkins with that attribute to carry their pumpkins into one circle. The students whose pumpkins don't have that attribute go into the other circle. Let students suggest another attribute and re-sort themselves, looking around to be sure they are in the right group. You may need to double-check at first. Continue for several more pumpkin re-shuffles. Play this game again at a later time to let your students practice classifying.

SUPERMARKET SORT

(center)
SUPPLIES: empty food boxes and cans with labels on them
EXPERIENCE: Arrange the grocery items on a shelf and encourage your students to sort these in as many different ways as possible. Be sure to allow time for kids to share their ideas. Then, work as a class to sort the items into food groups.

USING THE ACTIVITIES:

Reinforce your students' abilities to observe and give them needed practice in classifying with the activities on pages 47-49 (individual references, below). Kids will enjoy doing the worksheets, too! After looking at the activity pages, read the supply lists and practical suggestions given here.

PUMPKIN PATCH, page 47

(whole class and individual)
SUPPLIES: pencils, crayons, or markers
EXPERIENCE: To help your students understand how to do the classification exercises in this activity, draw a sample jack-o-lantern set on the chalkboard and let the class try to find the characteristic the set has in common. Hand out the "Pumpkin Patch" worksheet and have kids work in the same way on their own. After they finish the four sets, give them time to color the jack-o-lanterns.

LET'S EAT!, page 49

(whole class and small groups)
SUPPLIES: pictures of food, pencils, crayons or markers, scissors
EXPERIENCE: Prepare your students for this activity by talking about the four basic food groups. Use pictures to help kids identify the grouping of familiar foods. After practicing classifying in this way, divide your class into small groups. (Older children may be able to do this sheet on their own. Younger children may need more guidance.)

Lead each small group through the activity on page 49, while the other children are busy at learning centers. Discuss each meal and ask kids to tell you in which food group each lunchbox item belongs. Then ask which food group is missing from the meal. Encourage the students to pick a food that belongs to the needed group. When they are finished, let them color the meals.

Pumpkin patch

Decide what each of the sets of jack-o-lanterns has in common. Then draw a face on the blank pumpkin to make it part of the set.

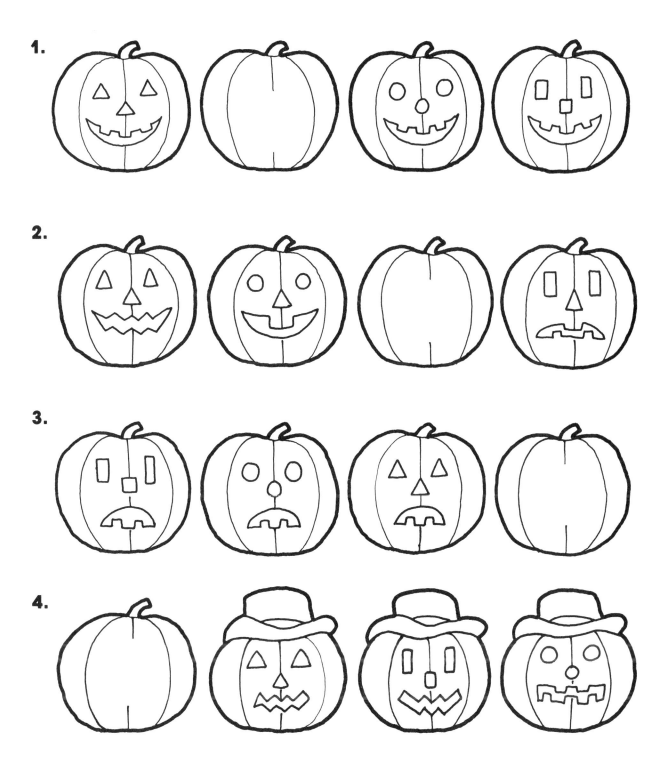

Jack-o-lantern Attribute card

Name _____

48

Let's eat

To feel good and have a lot of energy, you need to eat a well-balanced lunch. That means you need to eat something from each of the four food groups: 1. fruits and vegetables; 2. breads and cereals; 3. milk; 4. meats-eggs-nuts-beans.

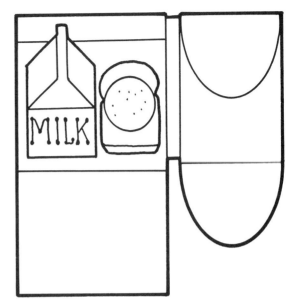

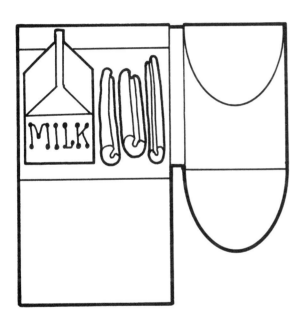

Cut out the food squares. Paste each one in a lunch box to make that lunch complete.

Name _____

NOVEMBER
Focusing on
Controlling Variables

2 Spruce Goose made its only flight in 1947
The 200-ton wooden flying boat built by Howard Hughes' aircraft company managed to rise 70 feet above the choppy water of Long Beach Harbor in Long Beach, California. It only stayed airborne long enough to travel about a mile. Many people were surprised that it even got off the ground. Give your students the activity "The Great Paper Airplane Race" on pages 57-58, to get them thinking about all the variables that need to be controlled for a successful flight.

3 John Montagu (England) born in 1718
He was the fourth Earl of Sandwich and he loved to gamble. So he created a time-saving meal that he could hold in one hand and munch without interrupting his game. Hence, the sandwich was born. Honor the earl and devote some time to this favorite food by turning to "The Hamburger Test" on pages 59-60. Your kids won't want to miss a chance to survey their friends' tastes by doing the activity "Sandwich Champ" on page 61.

8 X-ray discovered in 1895
This event launched a new era in medicine. Who discovered the X-ray? Wilhelm Conrad Roentgen (Germany). Arrange for a doctor, a dentist, or a local hospital to furnish several different X-rays. Display these in a window where the sun can illuminate them. Discuss how using X-rays helps doctors control variables when treating a medical problem. (It lets them see the usually hidden inside parts of the body so doctors can find abnormal conditions that may affect diagnosis and medical treatment.)

9 Christiaan Barnard (South Africa) born in 1922
This medical pioneer performed the first human heart transplant—providing new hope for many victims of heart disease. Help your students start their healthy heart program today. Ask them to control one of the heart-related vari-

ables discussed in class (see page 54). Give them the activity "You Gotta Have Heart" on page 62.

10 First commercial atomic energy reactor started producing power at Rowe, Massachusetts, in 1960

If possible, visit a nuclear-powered generating plant in your area. Have your students do research to discover how atomic energy is used to produce electricity. Also have them investigate the cause of the accidents at Three Mile Island (1979) at Middletown, Pennsylvania and Chernobyl (1986) in the Soviet Union. Have the class compile a list of variables that nuclear power plants must control to prevent such accidents (the rate at which the reaction happens, heat build-up, and treatment of radioactive wastes).

13 First artificial snow fell in 1946

Vincent Schaefer successfully created this fake snowfall by spreading dry-ice pellets from a plane at a height of 14,000 feet. He overlooked an important variable, though. The air was so dry that the snowflakes all evaporated before they reached the ground. Ready for a good winter activity? Just for fun, and a chance to think about controlling variables, challenge your students to see how long they can make ice last. As a guide, give them "Cold Challenge" on page 63.

15 Large scale use of Niagara Falls as a source of power began in 1896

The Robert Moses plant, which uses the energy of Niagara Falls to generate electricity, is one of the largest hydroelectric power stations in the world. Ask your students to find out more about how a hydroelectric plant operates. Have

them list what variables need to be controlled for it to function successfully (amount of water channeled from the falls and rate of flow—number of gallons per minute). Your students may be surprised to learn that the amount of water flowing over Niagara Falls is regulated.

25 The process of producing evaporated milk patented in 1884

This canned milk, which has about 60% of the water removed from it, was developed by John B. Meyenberg as a way of supplying pure milk that could be stored without spoiling. If possible, visit a fluid milk processing plant. Discuss with the class how variables can be controlled to successfully produce pure milk, that is milk free of disease-causing organisms (a sanitary environment for dairy cattle with disease-free cows, sanitary milking conditions, refrigerated storage of milk, a heating process—pasteurization—that kills disease-causing organisms, a sanitary bottling process, refrigerated storage, store checks for milk past its storage date and removal of that milk).

All month: Aviation History Month

This month honors the investigations made by the Montgolfier brothers, Joseph-Michel and Jacques-Étienne, in Annonay, France, during November, 1782. Their investigations, involving filling paper and cloth bags with hot air and smoke, led to the invention of the hot-air balloon and the science of aviation. Tell your students about the Montgolfier brothers. Then let them investigate what happens to air when it's heated, using the activity "A Lot of Hot Air" on pages 55-56.

Introducing Controlling Variables

Grades 3 and up

By the time your students become proficient at observing and classifying, they'll almost be ready to experiment. They need to learn to control variables to work the way a scientist would. Variables are those things that can change and affect the results of an experiment. To explain this simply, show them the results of two different experiments which you've conducted. The first experiment demonstrates what happens when variables are not controlled.

Display two different kinds of plants: a small, healthy plant in a big pot (labelled Plant A) and a larger, scrawny plant in a small pot (labelled Plant B). Explain that you wanted to find out whether water makes a plant grow taller. You gave Plant A enough water every day to keep its soil moist and you didn't give Plant B any water at all. You measured both plants daily for a week.

Plant A grew one-half inch taller, Plant B didn't grow at all. Point out that you are not sure whether it was the water or something else that affected the growth of the plant. Ask your students to help you identify all the other things besides water that might have caused the plant to grow taller. (They should name these possibilities: plant type, pot size, plant's health, and amount of soil. The kids may think of more.)

Tell your students that what they have listed are *variables*, those things which are varied or changed in an experiment. Explain that to collect meaningful results from an experiment, scientists must try to control the variables in exactly the same way—all treatments must be equal. (The acronym AOTBE, all other things being equal, is used by scientists to describe this.) Then the results which are observed are sure to be caused by the one thing, the variable, that was changed.

Present the class with your second experiment. This time you tried to control all possible variables: you used the same type of plants, pot size, amount and type of soil, and amount of light. The ONE THING you changed was the amount of water given to each plant. Present Plant C and Plant D. Plant C was given no water, Plant D was given water every day. Have students point out the differences between the two plants. Because all other variables have been controlled (AOTBE) you know it was the water which caused the growth of Plant D.

Now is a good time to introduce your students to the concept of control, which is needed in any experiment. The *control* is the object or group set aside in which nothing is changed or varied. Therefore, the control group exists as it would in nature. Because you do not vary anything, the experiment shows that what you have varied is different than what would happen naturally. For example, the control group in the second experiment was Plant C. You did not do anything to that plant during the experiment. It was allowed to exist as it would in nature. Thus, in comparing what has occurred, you can be sure that changing the variable—in this case, giving the plant water—was what made the plant grow.

EXTENDERS:

Identifying variables that could affect an experiment's results and figuring out how to control them is a skill your students will need lots of practice to develop. Ask them to list all the variables they can think of that would need to be controlled if they were to do each of the following experiments.
1. Testing to see if adding more wire coils makes an electromagnet stronger (type and thickness of the wire; lightness of the coils; type and size of metal core; type of test material to be picked up)
2. Testing to see whether adding fertilizer makes plants grow taller (type of plants; type of soil; pot size; number of plants per pot; room temperature; exposure to sunlight; amount of water)
3. Testing whether having a shorter string makes a pendulum swing faster (thickness of the string; type of string material that is used; way the string is tied to the support; size and heaviness of the pendulum; amount of force used to swing it)

As you discuss the results, teach your students one of the most important rules of experimenting in science: the result of any experiment conducted one time could simply be a freak occurrence. For reliable results, therefore, three repetitions of the same experiment are necessary. In addition, there should always be at least three control groups and three treatment groups. When an experiment shows the same or similar results at least three times, the findings can be counted on to indicate the expected outcome under the same conditions.

USING THE ACTIVITIES:

Now that the kids have gotten a taste of controlling variables, it's time for some intensive practice. The experiments on pages 55-63 will give your budding scientists a chance to get some of that practice within a carefully structured setting. However, making this process skill the natural part of experimenting that it needs to be will require more persistent effort. Individual page numbers for the experiments are given below so you can check them before you read the comments presented here.

A LOT OF HOT AIR, pages 55-56
(whole class and center)
SUPPLIES: two identical electric skillets, a pair of glass baby bottles, pairs of round rubber balloons in assorted sizes
EXPERIENCE: Give your students the first page of this activity to do, then discuss which variables should be controlled before kids perform the experiment. Put up a chart on which each child can record the measurements of his or her control and test balloons. Have each child do the test several times, then share results, just like scientists. When everyone has had a chance to perform the experiment, discuss the findings. You may want to have someone average the measurements that were recorded on the chart.

THE GREAT PAPER AIRPLANE RACE*
pages 57-58
(individual)
SUPPLIES: 8½'' × 11'' paper, scissors, tape, paper clips, index cards, a contractor's metal tape measure
EXPERIENCE: Arrange to use a section of a playground, a long hall, or a gymnasium as a flight range. Mark a starting point so everyone launches the planes from the same place. You may want to mark off feet to simplify how much measuring the children need to do. The planes can be expected to go long distances and measuring can become tedious work. Post class charts for the kids to record their longest control and test flights. You may want to award a certificate honoring the longest flight in each category.

THE HAMBURGER TEST, pages 59-60
(individual)
Have your students work on this activity at home. Stress that, as the instructions on their activity sheets state, they must work with an adult to do the experiment safely. Before the kids start, share the information about John Montagu (see page 50), whose birthday this activity is honoring, and about the origin of the sandwich. After the students have had time to experiment, allow them to share their results.

SANDWICH CHAMP, page 61
(individual and whole class)
Prepare your students for this activity by explaining how important it is to control variables for the reliability of survey results. You may also want to discuss national surveys and the efforts made by those conducting them to use a random sample. Having the kids visit other classes will make doing the activity more interesting and the results will be more than just a sampling of your students. Allow time to share results.
FOLLOW-UP: Challenge your students to create an original sandwich. Have them draw and color a picture of it, list the ingredients, and write step-by-step

*Challenging activity

directions for making it. Ask the children to think about what variables could affect how this sandwich will turn out.

YOU GOTTA HAVE HEART, page 62
(individual)
To introduce this activity, discuss things that are considered important for a healthy heart: avoiding smoking and alcohol, eating foods low in salt and cholesterol, avoiding too much stress, getting adequate rest and plenty of exercise. For free information and materials about living for a healthy heart, write to the American Heart Association National Center, 7320 Greenville Ave., Dallas, TX 75231. Consult your family physician or a nurse at a local hospital to research the best method to teach children how to take their pulse. To make pulse taking simpler, have the kids count their heartbeats for only 15 seconds and multiply this number by 4 to get the rate-per-minute.

COLD CHALLENGE, page 63*
(individual and whole class)
Challenge the kids to think and be creative by giving them this activity to work at home. Encourage them to use what they've learned about controlling variables as they experiment. Allow time for students to share their results in class.

*Challenging activity

A lot of hot air

Does hot air rise? When Joseph-Michel Montgolfier and his brother, Jacques-Étienne, experimented in 1782 to find out, their research led to the invention of the **hot-air balloon**—a giant bag that could be inflated with hot air and used to carry passengers in a basket that hung underneath. The following experiment, which uses a toy rubber balloon, will let you see what the Montgolfiers discovered.

Before you set up the experiment, decide what variables to control and how to control them. First, read the directions on page 56 to find out how the experiment works. Next, look at the list of variables. Circle the ones that have to remain the same in both the test and control parts of your investigation. Choose the supplies you will use to keep the circled variables uniform.

Variables

Size of skillet

Skillet's heat setting

Amount of water
    around the bottle

Balloon size and shape

Lighting in the room

Bottle size and shape

Volume of sounds in the room

Follow the directions on the next page. Then answer the questions about what you observed.

Name _____

To set up your own hot-air experiment, follow these step-by-step directions:

1. Take two electric skillets, one for the test and one for the control. Put a glass baby bottle in each skillet as shown at right.

2. Stretch the opening of a balloon over the neck of one of the bottles, then take another balloon and put it on the other bottle in the same way.

3. Make sure the dial is set on **off, then plug in the test skillet.** Leave the control skillet unplugged.

4. Pour water around the bottles. (During the experiment, you may have to add more water to the test skillet to keep it from going dry.)

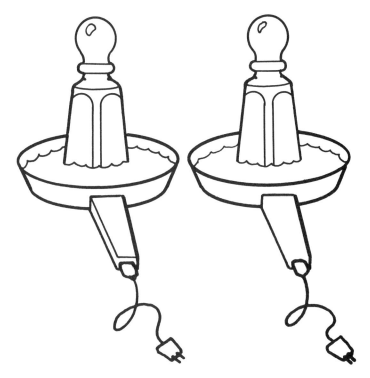

5. Turn the dial on the test skillet to **medium.** Observe the balloons after three minutes and after six minutes. Turn off the test skillet and answer these questions.

1. What did the test balloon look like after three minutes?

_____

2. What changes, if any, did you notice in the test balloon after six minutes?

_____

_____

The control balloon?

_____

_____

3. How many times should this experiment be repeated for the results to be reliable?

_____

4. Hot-air balloons must repeatedly use a burner to shoot a flame up into the open neck of the balloon. Based on what you discovered, explain how this procedure helps keep the balloon aloft.

_____

_____

56

The great paper airplane race

Here's your chance to see what it's like to be an aviation engineer. First, follow these step-by-step directions to build a standard paper airplane:

1. Fold a sheet of paper in half lengthwise.

2. Open the paper and fold corners A and B to the center crease.

3. Fold corners C and D to the crease.

4. Turn your airplane sideways as shown in diagram 4.

5. Fold the airplane in half to make it look like the one in diagram 5.

6. Now fold down the wings.

The airplane you've just built will be your control. Now choose which of the ideas in the Inventor's Box you will use to change the standard design when you construct your test model. (Or, be really creative and come up with a design change of your own.) Remember, your test model must differ from the control in only one way. Why is this important?

_____

_____

_____

_____

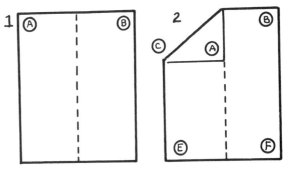

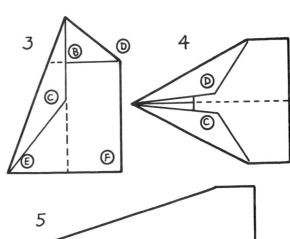

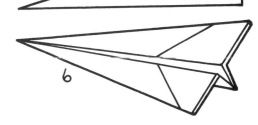

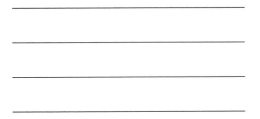

Inventor's Box

Add weight to the nose

Cut and fold up the wing flaps

Add a tail rudder

Add weight to the tail

Name _____

Describe the design change you made in your test plane.

_____

_____

Before you go to the test range, think about the variables.

1. What variables will you need to control as you fly your planes?

_____

_____

_____

2. Which of these variables will be the hardest to keep the same for every test flight?

_____

_____

3. Launch each of your airplanes three times and measure how far they fly. Write these distances on the chart.

Flights	**Control**	**Test**
1		
2		
3		

Based on what you discovered, how might you modify the change you made in your test airplane to get it to fly farther than it did?

_____

_____

Name _____

58

The hamburger test

Have you seen television commercials for hamburger restaurants that proclaim broiling is better than frying? The method of cooking which makes the meat taste better is a matter of personal opinion. But it is possible to test which causes a hamburger to lose more weight—frying or broiling. Find an adult to work with you. Then try this experiment. You'll need chopped meat, a frying pan, a broiling pan, a spatula, paper towels, and a kitchen scale.

First, prepare two hamburger patties that weigh exactly the same. Use the scale to check the weight. What other variables, besides weight, will you have to control as you prepare these patties?

_____

_____

Record the starting weight of each hamburger on the chart. Then place one patty in a skillet on the stove and the other in a broiler pan in the oven. Set the control dial on broil and turn the burner dial to medium. Cook each hamburger until the meat is no longer pink in the center of the patty. Then place the hamburgers on paper towels and let them set for five minutes. Reweigh and record the new weights on the chart.

Name _____

Cooking Method	Hamburger Weight	
	Before Cooking	After Cooking
Broiled		
Fried		

Which hamburger lost the most weight? _____

_____

Why should you repeat this test at least three times if possible? _____

_____

_____

_____

_____

Just for fun, unscramble the names of these familiar things to put on a burger.

1. hcektup   _____

2. ninoo   _____

3. esehec   _____

4. sduartm   _____

5. iceklp   _____

Name _____

60

Sandwich champ

Today sandwich making is an art. Sandwiches even have special names. There are gyros, hoagies, Dagwoods, and Reubens—just to name a few. Which sandwich is the most popular? You can take a survey to find out. First, list on the chart the names of the sandwiches you plan to include. Then, think about what variables you'll need to control so the results of your survey will be reliable.

How will you control the variables in this survey? Put an X in the correct box to show which sandwich the person surveyed liked best. Make a red X if a boy picks that sandwich and a blue X if a girl picks it.

Sandwiches	People Surveyed									
	1	2	3	4	5	6	7	8	9	10
1.										
2.										
3.										
4.										
5.										

Now use the survey to answer these questions.

1. Which sandwich was the boys' favorite? _____

2. Which did the girls like best? _____

3. Which was the all-around favorite? _____

The least liked? _____

Name _____

You gotta have heart

Exercise is important for a healthy heart. This experiment lets you find out what effect exercise has on your heart.

Your teacher has just demonstrated how to check your pulse rate. Sit very still for 5 minutes. Count how many times your heart beats in 15 seconds. Multiply that number by 4 to find your pulse rate for 1 minute. Record this number in the box next to *Quiet* in column 1 on the chart. Do this test two more times, recording the pulse rate each time.

Now make arm circles for 1 minute. Immediately after you've exercised, check your pulse rate as you did before and record the results in the correct box on the chart. Do this test two more times, sitting quietly for 5 minutes between each exercise period. Complete the chart, using the same testing method for the other exercises.

Heart Beats Per Minute

	Test 1	Test 2	Test 3
Quiet			
Arm circles			
Toe touches			
Jumping jacks			

1. What was the control in this experiment? _____

2. Why was it important to sit quietly for five minutes between each test?

_____

3. Why should you do the exercises at the same speed each time?

_____

4. Based on the results of this experiment, how does exercising affect your heart?

_____

_____

Name _____

Cold challenge
How long can you make an ice cube last?

Think about what affects the rate that an ice cube melts. Figure out what you can try to make the ice last longer.

1. What will you try? _____

2. List all the variables you will need to control your experiment.

_____

_____

You'll need six ice cubes: three for control cubes and three to test, a tape measure, and the supplies you need to test your variable. Measure the width of each cube and record these starting figures on the chart below. Record the cube widths after two-minute time periods. Write the measurements below.

Time	Control Cubes			Test Cubes		
Start						
2 mins.						
4 mins.						
6 mins.						

3. What variable was hardest to control during this experiment?

_____

Why?_____

_____

4. Based on your results, explain why this was, or was not, a good way to slow down melting?

_____

_____

Name _____

Especially for K—2

Introducing Sequencing

Once children have improved their powers of observation and learned to classify, the process skill they need to develop next is sequencing—arranging objects, people, or events in an orderly way. To introduce this skill, divide your class into two groups. Then challenge group members to arrange themselves in a line with the shortest at the front and the tallest at the back. Next, display objects that are different sizes. Call on your students to help you arrange these from biggest to smallest.

You may also want to have your students arrange pictures of people from youngest to oldest—for example, a baby, a toddler, an older child, an adult, and an elderly person. Have them arrange clear plastic bottles containing colored water in a sequence from the least to the most full.

To start your students thinking about the sequence of events in science experiments, perform this demonstration. Put one tablespoon of baking soda in a shallow bowl, pour on one tablespoon of vinegar, and observe what happens. Then ask your students to tell what you did first (put in the baking soda), second (added the vinegar) and what happened (saw the bubbling foam).

EXTENDERS:

THAT'S HEAVY
(center)
SUPPLIES: five or more 1/2-pint milk cartons, sand, masking tape
EXPERIENCE: Fill each milk carton with different amounts of sand. Seal the tops. Challenge your students to arrange these cartons in order from the lightest to the heaviest. To make this activity self-checking, number the cartons (but not in order). Post the correct number sequence somewhere else in the room.

WE'VE GOT RHYTHM
(whole class)
Start your students clapping slowly in a simple pattern; for example, hands together once, hands on legs once, then hands together twice. Repeat the pattern several times. Now have the class clap the pattern. Explain that when you stop clapping everyone is to stop. Continue the clapping pattern, then stop in mid-sequence and point to someone. This child has to complete the sequence for you and, if successful, becomes the leader. The child then teaches a new sequence to the class and tests the ability of the others to repeat it. If the child you point to misses the pattern, repeat the sequence twice, from the beginning, before challenging someone else.

WE DID IT
(center)
SUPPLIES: a camera, film, protective plastic sleeves (available at photo-supply stores)
EXPERIENCE: Take pictures of your students doing a special activity, such as cooking or drawing. Snap a photo just as everyone is starting and at various stages throughout the activity until it is completed. Number the backs of these pictures—but not in order—and slip them into protective plastic sleeves. Then put the set out for your students to arrange in order. Make this activity self-checking by displaying the correct number sequence somewhere else in the room. A photo selection center grows with the addition of pictures showing other sequence events. Store each series in a separate envelope. (The correct number sequence can be covered with a flap and used as a key). For kids learning to read, add a few sentences about each event to create a personal storybook your students will enjoy again and again. The sequences of pictures can be assembled into a class album and can be shared with parents at an open house.

USING THE ACTIVITIES:

Sequencing activities can be found on pages 66-68. Children in the K-2 range enjoy ordering things and events in their lives. Kids may want to create their own games to put things in order, using the following activities as models. Be sure to look at the activity sheets as you read the comments in this section.

WHO IS IT?, page 66
(whole class)
SUPPLIES: pencils, crayons, or markers
EXPERIENCE: Explain to your students that the numbers should be connected in sequence from the smallest to the largest to solve this puzzle. When they've finished, let them color their snails. You may also want to read them the story of a snail. One example is *The Biggest House in the World* by Leo Lionni (Pantheon, 1968), which is about a snail whose wish for a big fancy shell gets him into trouble.

WHAT'S MISSING? page 67
(small group)
SUPPLIES: scissors, glue
EXPERIENCE: This activity provides kids with practice in thinking about a sequence of events. They must depend on memories of observations to correctly complete the sequences. You may want to guide young children in small groups through this activity.

BUILD A SANDWICH, page 68
(whole class)
SUPPLIES: pencils, jars of peanut butter and jelly, bread, plastic knives, paper plates and cups, napkins
EXPERIENCE: Prepare your children for this activity by providing them with an opportunity to make peanut butter and jelly sandwiches. The steps listed on the worksheet can be used as a recipe. Explain the steps to follow in preparing this snack. After the kids finish making their sandwiches they may eat them.

Who is it?

This animal grows its own home to carry around. And it moves very slowly on just one foot, leaving a trail of shiny slime. Who is it? Connect the dots in order to find out. Start at the star.

Name _____

What's missing?

Cut out the squares at the bottom of the page. Then paste each square to complete a picture story.

Name _____

Build a sandwich

Number the steps, in the correct order, to make a peanut butter and jelly sandwich.

HIGHLIGHTS OF THE MONTH

DECEMBER
Focusing on
Inferring

13 U.S. satellite launched in 1962
The satellite, Relay I, began transmitting telephone and television signals after it was sent into orbit from Cape Canaveral, Florida. (It experienced a power failure after two days of operating.) Have your students watch a satellite-relayed television program in honor of this event. Ask kids to infer how the satellite helped them receive this program. (They may suggest the satellite bounced signals or received signals and transmitted them. Both answers are correct.) Have students do research to test their inferences (see also "Satellite Sort" on pages 32-33).

14 South Pole discovered in 1911
Who discovered it? (Roald Amundsen of Norway.) Display pictures of Antarctica so your students can observe what this continent is like. Then ask them to infer whether the trip to the South Pole was easy or difficult. Have them research this historic expedition to test their inference. Then have them use the information they discovered to write a newspaper-style account of the expedition.

17 First flight of a heavier-than-air craft in 1903
This event was the culmination of three years of experimentation with kites and gliders by the Wright brothers, Wilbur and Orville. Explain to your students how the Wright brothers observed the results of their experiments, made inferences and then experimented to test those conclusions. Orville piloted their first, controlled, powered airplane flight at Kitty Hawk, North Carolina. The flight lasted less than one minute but it was the beginning of a new age. (See also "The Great Paper Airplane Race" on pages 57-58.)

18 Antonio Stradivari (Italy), died in 1737
In honor of the man famous for making violins, listen to a musical piece featuring this beautiful instrument. Then let your students explore "Make Your Own Music" on pages 73-74.

19 Corrugated paper patented by Albert L. Jones (U.S.) in 1871

Which is stronger, plain or corrugated paper? Divide the class into small groups and give each group strips of plain paper and corrugated paper which measure 3 × 10 inches. Ask the kids to look at and feel the two papers and then infer which is the strongest. To test this inference, have each group lay the paper strips across two styrofoam cups that have been placed 4 inches apart and add pennies, one at a time, until the paper collapses. Have them repeat this test with the corrugated paper. Remind your students to conduct each test three times. (The corrugated paper will support many more pennies.)

21 Winter solstice

Post the official sunrise and sunset times for several weeks before this event. Ask your students to infer what is happening to the length of the day. Because of Earth's tilt, this day is the shortest of the year.

22 International Arbor Day

The traditional purpose of this day is to encourage planting trees on public lands. Arrange for your class to plant one on the school grounds. Then give your students the activity "Ring Reading" on pages 75-76.

25 Isaac Newton (England) born in 1642

Drop an apple and watch it fall in honor of this science hero. Newton supposedly was hit on the head by an apple falling out of a tree. His observation of this accident led him to infer that a force, gravity, pulled that apple toward the ground. Then Newton experimented to test his inference. Show your students pictures of astronauts weightless in space. Ask them to write a story, inferring what it would be like if Earth suddenly lost most, but not all, of its gravitational pull.

31 Electric light first demonstrated for the public in 1879

Who invented the first practical electric incandescent light? (Thomas A. Edison) Encourage kids to remember this inventor as they enjoy the colorful display of lights this year. Give them the activity "Holiday Lights" on pages 77-78. For those ready for a challenge, provide the activity "Light Puzzles" on page 79. See also "You Light Up My Life" on pages 38-39.

This month: Census of winter bird life begins

Devote recess to bird-watching in honor of what has been an annual event since 1900. Now, under the sponsorship of the National Audubon Society, more than 35,000 bird watchers count beaks in North America and Central America each winter. Give kids the activity "What's for Dinner?" on page 80.

70

Introducing Inferring
Grades 3 and up

Hold up a closed box that has a strong horseshoe magnet inside and touch a chain of steel paper clips to the bottom of the box below the magnet. The chain will stick to the box. Ask your students to explain why that happened. You'll probably get lots of suggestions. Write a number of them on the chalkboard.

Tell your students that scientists call an explanation of something observed an *inference.* Point out that as the class has just demonstrated, more than one is often possible. Help students understand how scientists use inferring as a problem-solving tool. Explain that when a scientist observes something happen during an experiment, he or she lists all the things that could possibly have caused it. Just like a detective trying to solve a crime, the scientist then has a list of "suspects" to check. The scientist does more experiments to test which of the inferences is the best possible explanation.

Did someone infer that the paper clips stuck to the box because the bottom is sticky? Then have a child test this inference by feeling the bottom of the box. It isn't sticky. Did someone suggest that there is something inside the box that attracts the metal clips? Insist that the box is sealed and can't be opened. Encourage your students to think about how they could test this inference. Lead them to decide that they could use another box that they can see has nothing inside and test whether or not it attracts the clips. They may also want to test whether the clips will stick to all parts of the box bottom or only to certain areas. Only the box with the magnet will attract the clips and only the area under the magnet will have any pull.

Summarize for your students that to use inference as a scientific tool they should follow these three steps:
1. Observe.
2. List all the possible inferences.
3. Make more observations to test those inferences.

EXTENDERS:

OUTSIDE SNOWY STORY
(whole class)
If it's snowy where you live, bundle up and go for a walk. When you find a place with tracks in the snow, ask your students to infer from the tracks what went on there. Was someone walking? Were children playing? Was one dog chasing another? What clues are students basing answers upon?

INSIDE SNOWY STORY
(whole class)
SUPPLIES: markers, three pieces of poster board or a transparency
EXPERIENCE: Draw three scenes of imaginary tracks, each on a separate piece of poster board or transparency. The first scene shows two sets of tracks heading towards each other. The second shows the tracks overlapping. The third scene shows just a single set of tracks. First, show only the poster with part 1. Based on the tracks they can observe, ask your students to explain what might have happened in this snowy field. Provide time for them to think and share their inferences. Then reveal part 2. Challenge kids to make new inferences based on these additional observations. Repeat, adding part 3.

USING THE ACTIVITIES:

The activities in this chapter, which appear on pages 73-80, help children to move from observing concrete things and events to inferring general rules and then seeing how these rules actually apply. Before you have kids do these activities, you may want to review the process skill of observing, which is important to inference making. After looking at the activity pages (references given below), read the instructions for teachers found in this section.

MAKE YOUR OWN MUSIC, pages 73-74
(individual)
SUPPLIES: enough medium-thick and thick rubber bands to give every child one of each (plus extras to replace those that break)
EXPERIENCE: Give kids this classroom activity to help them understand what affects the pitch of sounds. Your students shouldn't need much help from you as they work. The activity sheet carefully guides them through making an initial observation, using inference based on that observation, and then making further observations to test their inferences.

RING READING, pages 75-76
(individual)
EXPERIENCE: Have children do this simple activity to discover the practical applications of making inferences. Encourage them to think through the problem-solving situation carefully as they decide how to test their inferences.
FOLLOW-UP: Ask children to research additional changes in environment that can affect trees. Then have kids write the life story of a tree, including a picture of it and a close-up of the rings.

HOLIDAY LIGHTS, pages 77-78
(center)
SUPPLIES: a strip of aluminum foil, a cotton ball, a steel nail, paper, a wooden stick, a copper penny, an iron nail, a brass paper brad, a steel paper clip, an aluminum can, a yard of insulated copper wire, a D-cell battery, a 1.5-volt bulb, electrician's tape, a battery holder and a bulb holder (both are inexpensive and available at hobby stores that carry electronic supplies)

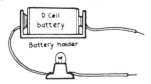

EXPERIENCE: To build a circuit tester, cut three 10-inch pieces of wire and strip about an inch of covering off the ends of each piece. Following the diagram, tape two wire ends to the battery holder and connect two to the bulb holder. Insert the battery and screw in the bulb.

LIGHT PUZZLES, pages 79*
(center)
SUPPLIES: two 8½″ × 11″ pieces of cardboard, aluminum foil, transparent tape or rubber cement
EXPERIENCE: Use two pieces of cardboard for each light puzzle. Following diagram 1, punch holes in one piece of cardboard and label them A through I. Cut out strips of aluminum foil the size needed for the connections shown. Cut out foil squares just big enough to cover the remaining holes. Use transparent tape or rubber cement to attach the strips and squares to the back of the hole-punched cardboard, positioning them as in the diagram. Then, back the puzzle with the other cardboard. Follow the same procedure for the second light puzzle, using diagram 2.

WHAT'S FOR DINNER?, page 80
(individual)
EXPERIENCE: Guide children through the observation-inference-observation process with this activity. To help students with the second part of the worksheet, you may want to use one of the birds in the list as an example to show kids how to compare beaks and find the mystery meal.
FOLLOW-UP: Have children make bird feeders that will attract birds to observe. *Invite a Bird to Dinner: Simple Bird Feeders You Can Make* by Beverly Courtney Crook (Lothrop, Lee & Shepard Books, 1978) is one source of directions for easy-to-build bird feeders.

*Challenging activity

Make your own music

When you play a tune on a musical instrument, you use different notes to create the melody. Some of the notes may be very high, some not so high, and others very low. The highness or lowness of a sound is called its **pitch**. You hear a sound because air is set in motion, vibrating. The faster the air vibrates each second, the higher the sound you hear.

Make a one-stringed "guitar" with a medium-sized rubber band. Slip it around a book so that it will fit easily and open the book's cover slightly, as shown. Pluck your guitar where the rubber band stretches between the front and back covers.

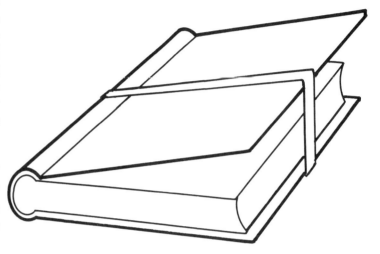

1. When you plucked the rubber band, was the sound low-, medium-, or high-pitched?

_____

2. Spread the cover open a little wider so the stretched section of rubber band is longer. Pluck the rubber band again. What happened to the sound?

_____

3. Now make an inference. Based on what you observed, explain what affects the pitch produced by a stretched rubber band.

_____

_____

4. How can you test your inference?

_____

_____

5. Try the test you planned. Then describe what you observe.

_____

Name _____

Does the rubber band's thickness affect pitch? Add a second rubber band string to your guitar and pluck it in all the ways you did the first one.

6. What happened to the sound when this rubber band was stretched longer and longer?

_____

_____

7. Were its sounds higher- or lower-pitched than those produced by the thinner rubber band? You may need to pluck the rubber bands one after the other to hear the difference between them.

_____

8. If you want to play deep notes on your guitar, what kind of rubber band string would you add?

_____

Why? _____

_____

Strike Up the Band!

Circle the twelve musical instruments hidden in this puzzle. The band box will show you what to look for. Check across, down, and diagonally.

```
G   U   I   T   A   R   U   M   S
C   L   A   R   I   N   E   T   O
V   V   E   O   T   U   B   A   B
T   H   I   M   P   L   P   X   O
S   A   X   O   P   H   O   N   E
F   R   O   B   L   L   L   M   P
L   P   D   O   V   I   B   A   I
U   D   R   U   M   T   N   C   A
T   E   C   E   L   L   O   D   N
E   T   R   U   M   P   E   T   O
```

Band Box

TRUMPET	DRUM	SAXOPHONE	HARP	PIANO	CELLO
VIOLIN	GUITAR	FLUTE	TUBA	CLARINET	OBOE

Name _____

Ring reading

An old tree stump is like a time capsule, displaying valuable information about the age of the tree and the climate in the past. Scientists have learned that every year a tree produces two growth rings—a light ring of rapid spring growth and a dark ring of slow summer growth. In very dry years, the rings are much narrower than in years with plenty of rainfall. The rings may even show scars that are evidence of a lightning strike or a forest fire.

Look closely at this tree cross-section . How old was the tree when it was cut? (Remember two rings are equal to one year's growth. To find the number of years, count only the light or dark rings.)

_____

_____

What can you infer about the weather during this tree's life?

_____

_____

_____

Name _____

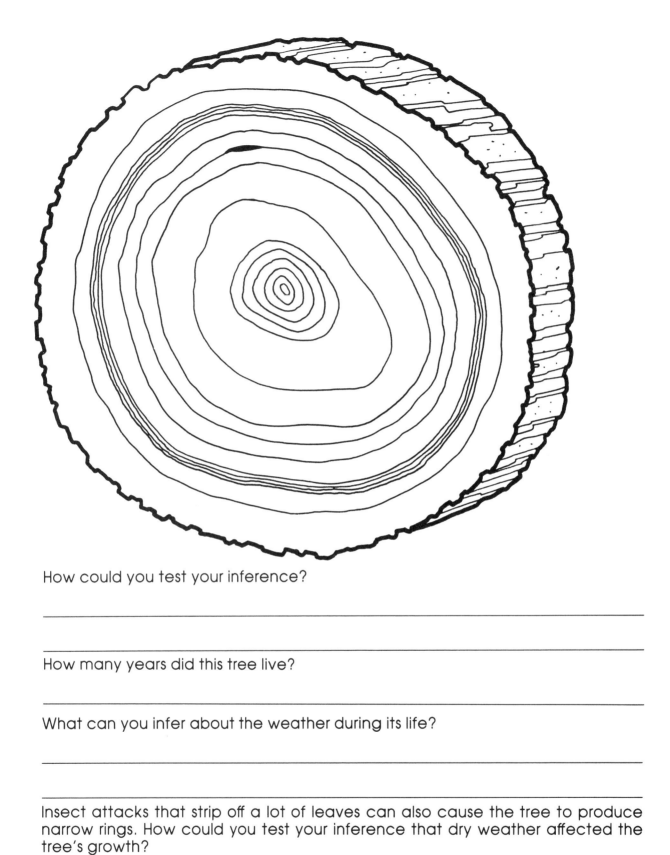

How could you test your inference?

_____

_____

How many years did this tree live?

_____

What can you infer about the weather during its life?

_____

_____

Insect attacks that strip off a lot of leaves can also cause the tree to produce narrow rings. How could you test your inference that dry weather affected the tree's growth?

_____

_____

Name _____

Holiday lights

Edward Johnson (a good friend of Thomas Edison, the inventor of the light bulb) had the first electric lights on his Christmas tree in 1882. There were no strings of lights back then. Even in 1895, when President Grover Cleveland first decorated the White House tree with electric lights, each bulb had a separate wire. Strings of lights weren't invented until 1907.

One bulb or one hundred—there has to be a **complete circuit** to make them light. The circuit is only complete when electricity flows from a power source, such as a battery, through the thin wire (the **filament**) inside the bulb and back to the power source.

Use the circuit tester your teacher prepared for you. Touch the two wire ends to the strip of aluminum foil. What do you observe?

_____

_____

_____

From this observation, you could infer that anything connecting the wires will complete the circuit. Test that inference by trying to complete the circuit with each item listed in the chart. After each test put an X in the appropriate column to show your results.

Test Item	Bulb Lights	Bulb Doesn't Light
Cotton ball		
Steel nail		
Paper		
Wood stick		

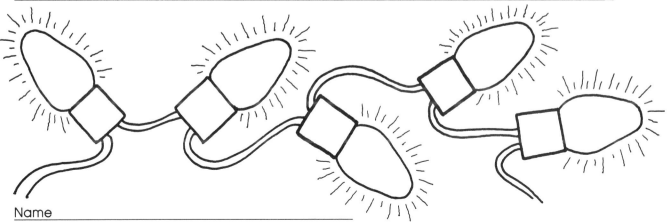

Name _____

You could infer that all metals will complete the circuit. To test this inference, use the items in the list below. Record your results on the chart.

Test Item*	Bulb Lights	Bulb Doesn't Light
Copper penny		
Iron nail		
Brass paper brad		
Steel paper clip		
Aluminum can		

*Be sure you test only shiny metals. Metals that are exposed to the air often form a coating called **oxide** on their surface. Oxide makes a metal look dull, and it changes the way the metal reacts to the flow of electricity.

Use what you learned to decide which of these two circuits will light the bulb. Color the bulb which can't be lit black.

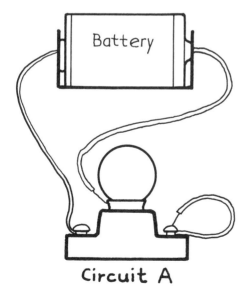

Circuit A

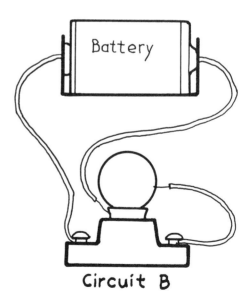

Circuit B

Name _____

Light puzzles

Your teacher has set up a circuit tester and prepared these two puzzles. Hidden aluminum foil strips connect some of the puzzle holes. If each wire end of the circuit tester touches the foil in a hole and the holes are connected, the circuit will be completed and the bulb will light. If the holes aren't connected, the circuit won't be completed and the bulb won't light. The instructions below on the left tell you which connections will make the bulb light and which won't. First, use this information to try out the holes and then to infer how the puzzles are wired. Draw lines on the puzzle diagrams to show the position of the foil strips.

1.

A to C = light

A to D = light

A to G = no light

C to G = no light

C to I = light

A	B	C
D	E	F
G	H	I

2.

A to C = light

A to G = light

C to G = light

C to I = no light

B to A = no light

A	B	C
D	E	F
G	H	I

Name _____

What's for dinner?

Wonder what a bird eats? You can usually tell by its beak. To learn how to make use of this clue, study the chart. Notice what shape beak each bird has, then read what kind of food it eats.

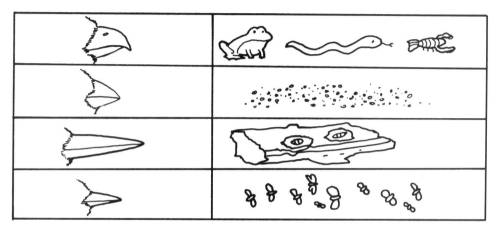

Now use your observations to infer which food the birds, shown below, would eat. Draw a line connecting each bird to its dinner.

Pigeon

Owl

Flicker

Bluebird

How could you find out if your inferences are correct?

Name _____

80

Especially for K-2

Introducing Inferring

Young children are quick to make guesses when you ask them to explain what caused something they observed. While they haven't yet learned many of the laws of nature that govern what specific results can be expected under certain conditions, they have already stored memories of many things they have observed happen. Now your students need to learn how to use that information to make inferences.

To introduce this skill, make up a mystery bag for each child by putting a half cup of popcorn into a lunch-size paper bag. Staple the top shut. Tell your students to shake the bag and listen. After everyone has had time to do this, call on several children to describe what they observed. Ask each one to suggest what could be inside the bag producing that sound. Encourage your students to use past information, and tell them to think about what they've heard before that sounded similar.

Explain that scientists call an explanation of something observed an *inference* and often more than one inference is possible. Then tell your students you want them to be scientists and make more observations to test their inferences. Next, tell the kids to gently feel the bag. Call for observations again and ask what the children think is in the bag. Also ask if what they inferred this time was the same as before or if they've changed their minds. If there has been a change, ask them why. Then have the children sniff the bag, make observations and revise their inferences. Finally, let everyone peek and eat the popcorn. You may want to expand this introduction to inferring by using picture activities. For example, show pictures of people in heavy coats, mufflers, and gloves. Ask the students to infer what the weather must be like. Repeat with pictures of people in shorts and bathing suits. You can use pictures to infer "What happens next?" Show a picture of someone at the top of a slide, someone swinging a baseball bat, or someone blowing out a candle. Ask the children to infer what action will occur next. Then ask them why they came to their conclusions.

EXTENDERS:

WHAT'S MY JOB?
(whole class)
SUPPLIES: a camera, film, clothing/costumes
EXPERIENCE: Let your students bring clothes and props from home to show themselves dressed for a specific job. Give the kids time in class to get dressed. Then have the children sit in a big circle and let each child stand up to be observed. (If a child's job isn't guessed right away, ask the child to pretend to be doing the job.) Finally, take a class picture of everyone dressed for work. Display the pictures on a bulletin board.

WHO LIVES WHERE?
(center)
Turn shoe boxes into dioramas—one for each of these habitats: lake, forest, and desert. (For older students you might include jungle and ocean.) Mount pictures of animals on index cards or use plastic animal figures. Tell your students that a habitat is a special home that provides food, temperature, oxygen, and living space that an animal needs.

Next, ask kids to place each animal in its habitat. This activity can be made self-checking by putting a colored strip on the back of each animal card (for example, have yellow represent desert; green, forest; and blue, lake).

USING THE ACTIVITIES:

On pages 83-85 are activities that provide an opportunity for kids to use past experiences to make inferences about present or future situations. Before students begin each activity, ask them to think about what they are basing their inferences on—what they have seen, done, heard, tasted, or felt before that helps them complete the activities. You'll find it helpful to read the comments for teachers given here, after you look over the activity pages.

LET'S PLAY!, page 83
(individual)
SUPPLIES: pencils, crayons or markers
EXPERIENCE: With this activity, help your students to infer the most likely destinations of people dressed in certain ways and to apply inferences in problem-solving situations. After kids finish, have them color the children and scenes.

FEELINGS SHOW, page 84
(individual and whole class)
SUPPLIES: pencils
EXPERIENCE: After your students have had a chance to do the activity page, discuss what observations led them to infer the feelings of the children in the pictures. Ask the students to tell you the ways they show these feelings. Encourage them to discuss what makes them happy, sad, and afraid.
FOLLOW-UP: Let your students take turns pantomiming different feelings for the class. Have the children in the audience guess each feeling.

WHAT HAPPENS NEXT?, page 85
(individual)
SUPPLIES: pencils
EXPERIENCE: With this activity, you give your students a chance to practice making inferences and to communicate those ideas. Arrange for the kids to present their inferences to an adult aide or older student volunteer. Then set up times that individual students can read their words to you.

Let's play

Draw a line from each child to the box that shows where he or she is going to play.

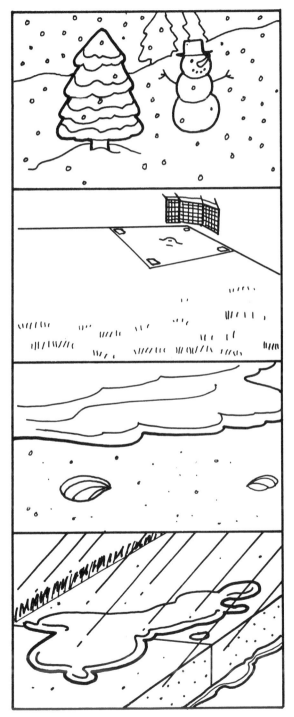

Name _____

Feelings show

Circle the word that tells how each child feels. In the last section, draw a picture to show how <u>you</u> feel right now.

1.

Happy   Sad   Afraid

2.

Happy   Sad   Afraid

3.

Happy   Sad   Afraid

4.

Name _____

84

What happens next?

Each of these pictures shows a child doing something. Below each picture, write a sentence telling what you think will happen next.

1.

_____

_____

2.

_____

_____

3.

_____

_____

Name _____

JANUARY
Focusing on
Communicating

HIGHLIGHTS OF THE MONTH

1 Radio broadcast first demonstrated in 1902

Have kids find out more information about this broadcast. In honor of the event, let groups in your class write radio plays, complete with sound effects. Tape the plays. Put the finished tapes at a listening center. This is also a good project to share with another class!

1 First coast-to-coast color television program broadcast in 1954

And what a colorful show! Viewer's lucky enough to have a color television in the twenty-one cities where this show aired were able to watch the Tournament of Roses parade in Pasadena, California, in all its natural beauty. Everywhere else, the parade appeared in black-and-white. Watch a color television program in honor of this broadcast. And give kids the activity "Coming to You Live" on page 90. Have your advanced students do research to find out what differences there are in the circuitry of black-and-white and color televisions.

4 Louis Braille's (France) born in 1809

This educator and inventor was born in Coupvray, France. He was blinded as the result of an accident when he was three. As a child, Braille studied at the Paris Institute of the Blind. He was particularly interested in science and music but found many of the materials he had to use there akward and cumbersome. In later years, he learned that the French army often sent messages at night using coded dots pressed into paper. Using this idea, Braille developed his own system which is two dots wide and three dots high. Combinations of dots in this pattern can produce 63 different characters, including letters, signs, and numbers! The Braille system has been translated into every major language and has even been used to produce games such as chess, bingo, and checkers! In Braille's honor, have your students do "Words You Can Feel" on page 91.

8 Telegraph invented in 1838
— — — — — •—• ••• •

That's Morse code for the name of the man who invented the telegraph. Give your students the activity "Talking Wire" on pages 92-93, and they'll be able to decode this inventor's name. Interested students may want to build their own telegraph. Directions are available in a number of books, including *Weather, Electricity, Environmental Investigations* by Sandra Markle (The Learning Works, P.O. Box 6187, Santa Barbara, CA 93111).

8 Herman Hollerith (U.S.) patented the tabulating machine in 1889

This machine was designed to count people for the census. It was also an ancestor of today's computer. Let your students celebrate its invention by counting some people, too. The activity "People Count" on pages 94-95, will guide them.

19 Neon tube electric sign patented in 1915

What a bright idea! Have kids research to discover how neon tubes are produced. (They are tubes filled with neon. The pure form of this gas gives off an orange-red light. To create other colors, neon must be mixed with mercury and other gasses or put into colored tubes.) Discuss with your class the uses of neon signs. Show them pictures or take them on a city tour to find samples. Ask your students to design their own signs that communicate messages showing brightly colored neon tubes.

24 Eskimo Pie patented by Christian K. Nelson (U.S.) in 1922

Let kids research what kinds of foods Eskimos really consider a treat during the icy Arctic winter. Have kids describe this ice cream treat and any other favorites. Then give them the activity "Pie? Oh My!" on page 96.

28 Piccard brothers (Switzerland) born in 1884

Auguste and Jean-Félix Piccard both made record-setting ascents in hot air balloons during the 1930s. Have each of your students write self-addressed, stamped postcards. Tie the postcards to helium-filled balloons and release them in honor of the Piccard brothers. Encourage kids to share any messages on returned cards and stick pins into a map to mark the places from which the cards were returned.

Introducing Communicating

Grades 3 and up

You may think your students use this process skill too much! However, kids need to learn to communicate effectively, to use precise language and provide meaningful observations, just as a scientist does. This introductory activity will help your students realize the importance of being precise and will help them clearly express ideas, directions, and feelings. It will also show them that it's useful to consider another person's viewpoint.

Start by dividing your class into pairs. Have each pair stand a file folder between them to create a wall, so they cannot see each other. Give them matching sets of tangram pieces or blocks. Next, instruct one member to create a design. It isn't necessary to use all the building pieces. Tell the kids to give instructions to their partners on how to arrange their pieces to create the same pattern. No fair peeking!

After each pair has had a chance to complete this activity, allow time for everyone to share what they found difficult about communicating the placement of the pieces. Lead your students to the realization that directions, such as left or right, were reversed from the partner's point of view. Very precise directions, such as north and south, were more meaningful. Encourage your students to suggest how to make directions easier to follow the next time. Have the partners switch roles and repeat the activity.

EXTENDERS:

WHAT IS IT?
(individual and whole class)
Have each of your students write a description of something in the room without naming it. Explain that descriptive phrases, such as *about the size of a ping pong ball,* are much more meaningful than adjectives like *small.* Have everyone read the descriptions aloud one at a time. Challenge the other students to guess the mystery object. Ask your students to write step-by-step directions for completing a familiar task, such as making their beds or tying their shoes. Have them try to perform

the tasks at home, following their own directions—doing only what the steps state. Allow time in class for students to share what difficulties, if any, they encountered in writing the steps.

Explain that detailed directions are important when scientists repeat experiments. Because experiments must be done over and over to see if the same or similar results happen each time, scientists need to provide a precise description of an experiment's results, too. Knowing exactly what happened lets other scientists evaluate how the information gathered can be used.

USING THE ACTIVITIES:

The activities on pages 90-96 focus on the process skill of communicating. After your students do each activity, encourage them to continue working with the form of communication featured in it. Have the kids share these additional messages or descriptions with their parents. You may also want to send home a letter to involve parents or special adults in their children's efforts to learn to communicate effectively. Individual references for the activities appear below.

COMING TO YOU LIVE, page 90
(individual)
SUPPLIES: crayons, colored pencils or paints
EXPERIENCE: Prepare your students for this activity by compiling a class list of adjectives and comparative phrases that could be used to describe the beautiful floats. Let the children select materials to use to color the float picture. Display the pictures along with the descriptions.
FOLLOW-UP: Have your students work in small groups to make cardboard box floats. Let each group decorate their float with tissue paper flowers, crepe paper draperies, and so forth, and attach a string to pull it. Have everyone join in a classroom parade! Afterwards, ask the children to write a description of this special event.

WORDS YOU CAN FEEL, page 91
(individual)
EXPERIENCE: Have your students find out more about Louis Braille's life—it's an inspiring story. You might also want to invite a speaker from your local association for the blind to show the class Braille books and talk about the needs of the blind. It would be great for your students to share their sight by reading to someone who is blind or vision-impaired.
FOLLOW-UP: Discuss the importance of good eye care. Explain the function of protective eyewear and stress the need for regular eye examinations. You might also want to arrange for an optometrist to come and tell the class about what goes on during an eye examination.

TALKING WIRE, pages 92-93
(individual and whole class)
Discuss how the telegraph greatly increased people's ability to communicate over long distances. When the children finish the activity, have them exchange messages to practice decoding. Then let the kids take their messages home and try sending them with a flashlight, using short blinks for dots and long ones for dashes.

PEOPLE COUNT, pages 94-95
(individual and whole class)
SUPPLIES: enough index cards to give six to each child, hole punches, pipe cleaners

EXPERIENCE: Explain that a survey is a way to collect and communicate information about a lot of people. Have the kids set up their cards and tabulate results in class. Be sure to review safety rules for using scissors before students gather their information. You may want to expand "People Count" by using the same method to do another survey. This time have the kids write yes-or-no questions of their own. Discuss the difficulty of compiling information given by the thousands of people in a typical sample. Lead your students to the conclusion that this is a job computers handle very well. Ask the kids to research the role of computers in evaluating election polls, counting ballots, and predicting election results.

PIE? OH MY!, page 96
(individual and whole class)
EXPERIENCE: To prepare your students for putting this list of directions in order, guide the class through creating a set of steps for cooking something simple, such as scrambled eggs. You might also want to bring in some cookbooks containing easy recipes so kids can look at the directions and see how these are written.
FOLLOW-UP: Have the children ask a parent or special adult how a favorite dish is made and write directions for it. Then, with the help of the adult, have them try this recipe in the kitchen. Allow time for the kids to share their experiences in class.

Coming to you live

The Tournament of Roses in Pasadena, California, was the first color program broadcast on television. But a lot of people still had to watch on black-and-white sets, which meant that it was still necessary to imagine the event's many colors based on what the announcer described.

Pretend that you are the announcer. How do you describe those fabulous flowered floats so you can share the colors with *all* of your viewers? On a separate sheet of paper, draw and color a picture of a float. In the space below, write a description of the float.

Name _____

Words you can feel

At one time, books for the blind had special raised letters. The letters had to be at least three inches high for fingers to trace them, only a few words could fit on a page. The books were extremely big and sentences went on for pages and were hard to read. Then, Louis Braille invented an alphabet of raised dots—based on sets of six dots arranged in two columns. These dot-sets were easy-to-feel and could be read when small. The set also has punctuation signs and 189 special word symbols. With Braille's invention, books for the blind could be made which were compact and had many words on each page.

Make a Braille alphabet.

Each set of six dots you see below stands for a letter. Put a pad under this sheet. Using a pen or pencil, gently press each dot. Turn the page over and label each letter. "A" will be in the upper left, "J" on the upper right. Now read the alphabet by moving your index finger over the raised dots, from left to right.

j i h g f e d c b a

t s r q p o n m l k

z y x w v u

What musical instruments can you find in your ears? Press the dots, turn the paper over, and use your fingers to read the answer to this riddle in Braille.

Name _____

Talking wire

That's what the Indians called the telegraph. The telegraph wire doesn't really talk, of course, but people do use it to send messages. This is done by pressing a key, which completes an electric circuit. This creates an electromagnet at the opposite end of the line and pulls a piece of metal down with a click. Samuel F. B. Morse, the inventor of the telegraph, also developed a system of dots and dashes—Morse code—to send messages using these clicks. Look at the alphabet in the box to find out how to represent letters in Morse code.

Morse Code

The answer to this riddle is in Morse code. To decode it, match the dot-dash groupings below to ones in the box.

A • —   G — — •   L • — • •   Q — — • —   V • • • —

B — • • •   H • • • •   M — —   R • — •   W • — —

C — • — •   I • •   N — •   S • • •   X — • • —

D — • •   J • — — —   O — — —   T —   Y — • — —

E •   K — • —   P • — — •   U • • —   Z — — • •

F • • — •

What stays hot no matter how cold it gets?

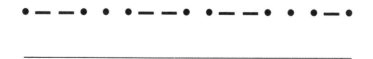

_____

When Morse first began operating a telegraph service, people were amazed and thrilled by the opportunity to send messages almost instantly over long distances. They didn't always understand how the telegraph worked, however. One woman asked Morse to send, but not to read, a letter to her boyfriend! That, of course, was impossible because he had to read her message and change it into code in order to transmit it. Longer messages cost more to send, too. People had to make messages clear but brief if they were to be sent by telegraph.

Follow these steps to write a message of your own to send in Morse Code.

1. Think of something that has happened to you that you wish to share with someone, a friend or perhaps a grandparent living far away. Write a detailed description of what happened.

2. Rewrite your message, condensing it into 25 words or less. Reread it to be sure this shortened message still communicates the feelings and events you want to share.

3. Rewrite your message in Morse code, leaving space between letters and extra space between words and sentences.

Name _____

People count

By 1880, computing the United States census (a count of how many people lived in this country and a record of different facts about them) had become very time-consuming. Totaling the numbers for the 1880 census took seven years! A contest was held in 1890 to see if someone could find a better way to do the job.

Herman Hollerith won. He invented a system that used punched cards to record answers for the census survey. These cards were placed in a tabulating machine, which read them one at a time. Wherever there was a hole in the card, a little metal pin dropped through, completing an electric circuit. Each completed circuit caused one of the machine's dials to add one more to its total. Thanks to Hollerith's invention, the results of the 1890 U.S. census were announced after only six weeks.

You can use punched cards to quickly take a survey of your own. First, write the numbers 1 through 6 on a 3 x 5 index card, as shown. Use a hole punch to punch a hole between each number and the edge of the card. Use this card as a pattern to punch holes in five other cards. Number the holes 1 through 6 as before.

Find six different people to survey and use a card for each person. Write each person's name in the middle of a card. Ask the questions listed on the next page and record the answers. First, match the number of the question with the number of the hole in the card. If an answer is yes, don't do anything. If the answer is no, use scissors to cut open the top of the punched hole as shown.

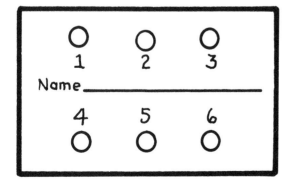 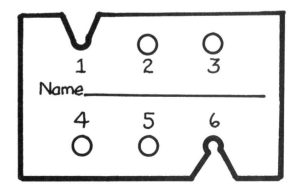

Name _____

What's Your Favorite?

1. Do you like vanilla ice cream best?

2. Is an apple your favorite fruit?

3. Would you rather have a dog than any other kind of pet?

4. Is popcorn your favorite snack?

5. Would you rather play soccer than any other sport?

6. Is Saturday your favorite day to watch TV?

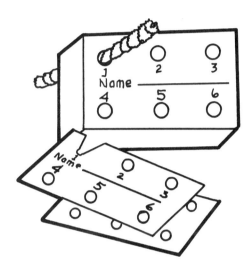

To find out how many people in your survey like vanilla ice cream best, stack the cards together, put a pipe cleaner through the first hole, and shake. The cards of those who don't like vanilla ice cream will fall out. Count how many cards are left hanging on the pipe cleaner. Use this method to tabulate the results, and record the number of yes answers in the correct column on the chart.

Number of People Who Said Yes					
Vanilla	Apples	Dogs	Popcorn	Playing Soccer	Saturday TV

Pie? oh my!

Here are the directions for making a homemade ice cream pie. The steps are out of order, so they don't communicate what you really need to do to make this treat. Think about when each task should be done. Then, number the directions to show what should be done first, second, third, and so forth.

Spread the ice cream on one half of the cake. _____

Get all the ingredients. _____

Cut into squares. _____

Let the vanilla ice cream soften slightly. _____

Divide the cake in half. _____

Let the cake cool. _____

Mix the dough for the chocolate cake. _____

Bake the cake. _____

Place the other half of the cake on top of the ice cream. ____

Now write directions for making your favorite ice cream treat in five steps.

_____

_____

_____

_____

_____

Try your directions out on a friend or family member. Are your communications clear?

Name _____

96

Especially For K-2
Introducing Communicating

Kids love to talk! They also need to learn how to express ideas effectively. A good way to start your students thinking of communicating as a process skill is with this demonstration. It's best when done in small groups. Work with about four children at a time while the others are at learning centers. For this activity, you'll need a jar of jelly, a jar of peanut butter, a loaf of bread, a knife, and a plate. After the kids have washed their hands, have them come to a table where you've arranged the food and other items. Explain to the children that you're going to make a peanut butter and jelly sandwich, and you want them to tell you how to do it. Ask one child how to begin and follow his or her directions literally. For example, if you are told to put the peanut butter on the bread but not to take out a slice of bread or open the peanut butter jar, put the jar on top of the loaf. They will quickly—and delightedly—tell you that you're wrong. Act surprised and ask for new instructions. Encourage the children to think through what needs to be done and give you specific step-by-step directions. Reward the kids by slicing the finished sandwich and dividing it among them. Repeat this activity with the other groups.

Expand on the development of this skill, and practice distinguishing right from left, with this path-finding activity. Start by marking a path on the floor with masking tape. Be sure the path has several right-angle turns.

Next, remind your students how remote-controlled toys are directed from a distance. Stand at the beginning of the path and say that you are now remote-controlled and will follow their directions. Explain to the kids that to make you move they must tell you what direction to go—forward, backward, right, or left—the number of steps to take. Call on one student at a time and move, robot-like, exactly as the child tells you. Later, let your students take turns being remote-controlled.

EXTENDERS:

SIMON SAYS
(whole class)
To help kids listen and follow directions, play this familiar game. Explain to the children that when the leader tells them "Simon Says," everyone must do what the leader says. Let different children take turns being the leader.

HAND SIGNALS
(whole class)
The special hand signs used to communicate with the hearing-impaired are easy to learn. (Is there someone in the community who can visit and share this language with the class?) You may also wish to teach your students some traditional Indian signs. One source of these is The Official Boy Scout Handbook.

CAN YOU SEE WHAT I FEEL?
(center)
SUPPLIES: paper, water, tempera paints, brushes
EXPERIENCE: A picture can express feelings, too. Set up a painting center and encourage your students to create a happy picture. This makes a good finger painting activity. Display the pictures. Let the children tell what makes their pictures happy. Later, you may want to have the children paint a sad picture.

USING THE ACTIVITIES:

Before you read the tips and instructions in this section, look at the activites on pages 99-102 (individual references are given here). These worksheets are designed to help your students learn to communicate more effectively. Each activity features a practical way of communicating that children must master for daily living. After the kids complete the activities, create similar worksheets of your own, since continued practice is advisable.

PLEASE WRITE BACK SOON, page 99
(individual)
SUPPLIES: pencils
EXPERIENCE: Help your students decide to whom they wish to write. Show them how to address an envelope so they can mail the letters they write. Encourage the children to share any replies they receive with the class.

THE FUNNY PUPPY, pages 100-101
(small groups)
SUPPLIES: pencils, crayons, or markers
EXPERIENCE: Divide your students into small groups for this activity. Then work through the activity with one group while the others are busy in learning centers. Allow time for each child to communicate what he or she sees happening in the pictures. After the kids talk about a picture, you may want to let them make up their own sentences which communicate the action they've described. Guide them in rearranging the scrambled sentence. Help them to realize that the number of blanks in a word group is a clue to what word fits in that spot. You will also want to point out the period that signals the end of a sentence. Have the children color in the puppy pictures after they finish.

HELP ME LEARN TO USE THE TELEPHONE, page 102
(individual)
SUPPLIES: play telephones
EXPERIENCE: Help your students learn to use an important communication tool by giving them this activity which encourages parental involvement. Demonstrate correct dialing procedures in the classroom. Set up a telephone center with several play telephones so the children can practice dialing and calling each other. Give each child an imaginary three-digit telephone number and have them call each other's numbers at the center.

Please write back soon!

Fill in the blanks to complete this letter. Cut along the dotted line and mail it.

_____ , 19_____

Dear _____,

   Today the weather is _____

_____.

When the weather is like this, I like to _____

_____.

The thing I like to do best at school is _____

_____.

Sometimes, it's fun to _____

_____.

When I play outside at school I really like to _____

_____.

   Please write to me soon. I would like to hear from you.

          Love,

_____

Name _____

The funny puppy

You can tell a story about the funny puppy. Look what is happening in the first picture. Use the words below each picture to make up a sentence about what happened. Write your sentence in the blanks. Do the same thing with each of the other pictures on these two pages. Take your story home and read it to someone.

ball his after Puppy ran

_____

helped Billy his Puppy ball get

_____

Name _____

100

all muddy got Puppy

_____

Puppy gave Then Billy bath a

_____

Name _____

Help me learn to use the telephone

Dear Parent or Guardian:

   The telephone is one means by which your child can get assistance in an emergency. A telephone conversation is a nice way to talk to someone special, like a grandparent. Please help your child answer these questions and practice using this essential communication tool.

1. My telephone number is _____

2. If I want to make a call, I listen for the _____.

   I then dial or press the numbers slowly.

3. If the line is busy, I will hear a busy signal. Then I should _____

   _____

4. When I call on a pay phone, I first need to _____

   _____

   Next, I should listen for the _____

   I can then dial or press the numbers slowly. If I don't get an answer, my

   money _____

5. If I don't have any money and need to use a pay phone to get help, I

   can dial or press _____ to reach the operator.

6. When I answer the telephone at home, I should say _____

   _____

Name _____

HIGHLIGHTS OF THE MONTH

2 Groundhog Day
This furry creature can supposedly predict how many more weeks of winter there will be. How does the groundhog make its prediction? (If the groundhog sees its shadow on this day, there will be six more weeks of winter.) Is the prediction reliable? Although this is only a weather myth, finding out about what the groundhog does or doesn't see can be fun. Ask your students to investigate the history of this myth.

9 The United States Weather Bureau authorized in 1870
Record weather information on a calendar all month in honor of this event. Check how close the actual weather conditions are to what is predicted for each day.

10 Fire extinguisher patented by Alanson Crane (U.S.) in 1863
Arrange for a firefighter to discuss fire safety and demonstrate how a fire extinguisher works. Then give your students the activity "On Fire" on pages 107-108.

14 Solar Max launched in 1980
This satellite, whose official name is Solar Maximum Mission Observatory, was designed to study the sun from a vantage point high above the Earth's atmosphere. Shortly after it was launched, four of its seven scientific instruments failed. Normally, such failure would mark the end of a satellite's usefulness. However, in 1984, astronauts aboard the space shuttle gave Solar Max new parts and made it the first satellite to be repaired in space. For information about what patterns of solar activity this satellite has observed, write to the NASA Center (National Aeronautic and Space Administration) nearest you. Ask your students to do the activity "For Sun Watchers" on page 109.

15 Pilot plant for producing artificial diamonds built in 1955
Ask your students to research why industry considered diamonds so important and why the production of artificial ones was a welcomed

FEBRUARY
Focusing on
Predicting

advance. (The hardness of diamonds made them ideal for use in drilling and grinding machines, such as an oil well drill and a dentist's drill. But the cost of using real diamonds was expensive.) The General Electric Company produced the artificial diamonds by subjecting carbonaceous compounds to pressures of 1.5 million pounds per square inch (6¼ square centimeters) at a temperature of 2,760° C (5,000° F). Let kids explore the activity "Crystal Clear" on pages 110-111.

18 Pluto discovered in 1930
How was this planet found? Dr. Percival Lowell predicted that Pluto had to exist. Then, using mathematical computations based on the orbital patterns of known planets, he showed where in the solar system it should be located. Pluto was first observed by Clyde W. Tombaugh at the Lowell Observatory in Flagstaff, Arizona, continuing the systematic search Dr. Lowell had begun. New information about Pluto is being discovered all the time. Ask your students to research what special features astronomers have learned about Pluto.

19 Thomas A. Edison (U.S.) patented the phonograph in 1878
Listen to a record in his honor. (Also see "Make Your Own Music" on pages 73-74.)

21 First telephone directory issued in New Haven, Connecticut in 1878
Have kids use the telephone yellow pages to locate where in their community they can eat Chinese food, find help for a sick pet, find a new tire for someone's car, and watch a movie. For more telephone directory skill-building, give your students "In the Phone Book" on page 112.

24 Synthetic bristles for toothbrushes first produced in 1938
Ask students to predict what a dentist would say are the five most important rules for children their age to know. Arrange for a dentist to visit. Have that person share information about the relationship between good brushing habits and healthy teeth and gums.

Introducing Predicting

Grades 3 and up

Kids have probably heard people make predictions about the future. They need to understand that many times these are just guesses. Explain that to be a useful scientific tool, predicting must be based on a reliable pattern. In fact, recognizing a pattern is the whole key to making predictions.

Divide your class into pairs and give each pair a marble, a book, and a strip of tape. Have the children work on the floor in a place with plenty of room, such as a gymnasium. Tell your students to tip the book slightly and release the marble at the top of this incline. Ask them to use a small piece of tape to mark how far the marble rolls. Have them repeat this experiment, inclining the book a bit more steeply, and observe how far the marble rolls this time.

Have the pairs share their results. Ask your students what patterns they see developing. Guide them to the conclusion that the more steeply the book is inclined, the farther the marble rolls. (This is true up to the point that the book is nearly vertical.) Then ask the children to predict what effect starting at the top of an even steeper incline will have on how far the marble rolls. They should predict that the steeper incline will make the marble roll even farther. Have your students test this prediction to encourage their confidence in using patterns to make predictions.

Besides predicting future results, predictions are also useful for making estimates. For example, how many blades of grass are on a football field? Counting the blades of grass would be difficult and time-consuming, if not impossible.

Explain to your students that to establish a pattern for predicting large quantities, they can follow these three steps:
1. Count how many of the things are in each of several small samples.
2. Compute the average number in a sample, by dividing the total by the number of samples.
3. Determine how many samples would be in the whole.
To demonstrate, have small groups count how many raisins there are in a one-ounce sample of raisin bran cereal. (Use a kitchen scale to weigh the cereal and put the

samples in self-sealing plastic bags.) Next, let the groups share their results and compute a class average for the number of raisins in a one-ounce sample. Finally, ask your students to predict, based on this pattern, how many raisins they can expect to find in a 16-ounce box and a 32-ounce box of the cereal.

The kids can try predicting at home, too. Have them work on how many chocolate chips are in a box of chocolate chip cookies or how many leaves are on a tree.

EXTENDERS:

WEATHER FORECAST
(whole class)
SUPPLIES: copies of a table showing yearly rainfall statistics for your community
EXPERIENCE: Ask your students to infer a pattern from the table and challenge them to predict whether to expect a lot, a medium amount, or only a little rain next month. Have each child keep a weather calendar to check the accuracy of his or her prediction.

THE WHOLE GROWTH PICTURE
(whole class and homework)
SUPPLIES: copies of a chart showing average growth patterns for children
EXPERIENCE: Have each student create a fictional person and graph the person's growth. Then ask the kids to use this pattern to predict future growth. Send a copy of the chart home so parents or special adults can work with the kids to graph their own growth.

USING THE ACTIVITIES:

Activity pages 107-112 emphasize the process skill of predicting. These worksheets also give your students an opportunity to examine some aspect of their environment. You might want to expand each investigation by inviting a speaker who works in a related field. Individual page references have been included in this section. Examine the activities before you read the instructions given here.

ON FIRE, pages 107-108*
(whole class)
SUPPLIES: modeling clay, three birthday candles, matches, a metal cookie sheet, a pint jar, and a quart jar
EXPERIENCE: This activity gives your students a chance to look for a pattern as they observe the results of an experiment and use the pattern to solve a problem. To be done safely, the experiment should be presented as a demonstration. Your students can answer the questions as they observe the results. In preparation for the experiment, you'll need to make three quarter-size balls out of modeling clay. Place them in a row on a metal cookie sheet, spacing them as far apart as possible. Stick one candle in the center of each clay ball. Talk to your students about working safely with fire. Point out that as a safety precaution, it is important to have a very wet paper towel ready to place over a burning candle to quickly put out a flame. Now light the candles and put a pint jar over the first one and a quart jar over the second. The third candle is uncovered. When these two candles go out, blow out the remaining one.

FOR SUN WATCHERS, page 109
(homework)
Have your students build their confidence in predicting with this easy-to-do activity, which includes tasks such as collecting information and looking for a pattern to use in answering questions. Let the kids compare their results in class.

CRYSTAL CLEAR, pages 110-111*
(small groups)
SUPPLIES: laboratory equipment for each group: a measuring cup, a tablespoon, a mixing bowl, a glass or clear-plastic container with sides at least 3 inches/7¼ centimeters high (if nothing else is available cut off the bottom of a plastic soft-drink or milk bottle), pieces of broken brick or charcoal briquettes, salt, laundry bluing, ammonia, food coloring, and water
EXPERIENCE: Give your students this activity to help them learn to recognize and apply a pattern from nature. Before the kids start the experiment, tell them ammonia is poisonous and to be careful in pouring it. Point out that if some gets on their hands, they should wash it off right away. After the activity, have each group share how their garden turned out.

IN THE PHONE BOOK, page 112
(center)
SUPPLIES: your area's residential phone directory
EXPERIENCE: Have your students do this activity to learn how to use predicting as a tool in a real-life problem-solving situation. Be sure to emphasize that only full pages of names should be used for the sample survey. After the kids finish the activity, have them compare their totals. You might want to use this worksheet as a homework assignment instead of a science center activity.

*Challenging activity

On fire

A fire needs oxygen to burn. How long will a candle stay lit inside a closed gallon container? To help you find out, your teacher is going to do an experiment with three candles. When they are lit, write the time on the chart. Watch closely and record the time whenever a candle goes out. Subtract the time the candle went out from the time it was lit to find out how long it burned. Record this number on the chart. If your teacher blew out the candle, leave the **Length of Time Burned** box blank.

Candle	Lit	Goes Out	Length of Time Burned
1			
2			
3			

Name _____

Make a graph of the results you recorded on the chart on page 107. Color the correct number of spaces to show how long a candle burned in each amount of oxygen.

Minutes burned

5 _____

4 _____

3 _____

2 _____

1 _____

0 _____

Amount of
oxygen available

1 pint   1 quart*
(480 milliliters)   (960 milliliters)

*Equal to 2 pints.

1. How many pints are there in a gallon?

_____

2. How many minutes do you predict a candle will burn in a closed gallon container?

_____

3. How many minutes do you predict a candle will burn under a container that is bigger than a pint but smaller than a quart jar?

_____

4. Which of these two predictions do you feel more confident about?

_____

Why? _____

_____

_____

Name _____

For sun watchers

During the period of a day, the sun seems to change position in the sky. But the sun isn't really moving; Earth is. As Earth spins, places on its surface face different directions. During the daytime, the area where you live is turned toward the sun. At night, your area is turned away from the sun. Because of the way Earth tilts and moves along its orbital path around the sun, the exact moment of sunrise and sunset changes slightly each day. Can you predict when sunset will be?

You'll need a pencil and a radio, a television, or five issues of a daily newspaper for Monday through Friday of one week. Use the radio, television, or newspapers to find out the official sunset time for each day of the activity. Record this information on the chart.

Sunset time for the week of _____ to _____

Day	Sunset Time
Monday	
Tuesday	
Wednesday	
Thursday	
Friday	

Look for a pattern in your observations and use it to make the predictions called for in the questions below.

1. Predict when sunset will occur on the Saturday right after your recorded week.

_____

2. How confident do you feel about this prediction?

_____

_____

3. Predict the sunset time for the following Saturday.

_____

4. Did you feel confident using the chart to make the prediction?   ☐ Yes   ☐ No

Why? _____

_____

Name _____

Crystal clear

How are crystals formed? First, hot liquid rock, deep within the earth, begins to rise. As it nears the surface, this molten material cools and solidifies. The molecules arrange themselves in geometric patterns called **crystals.** The slower the liquid rock cools, the more time there is for crystals to form and grow. Look at these two rock samples. The granite cooled slowly while the basalt cooled quickly.

Which rock has more crystals?

Which has larger crystals?

_____

Here's another rock for you to examine. How quickly did it cool?

☐ very quickly

☐ quickly

☐ slowly

☐ very slowly

_____

**photos courtesy of Wards Natural Science Establishment, Inc.)

Name _____

Why did you come to this conclusion._____

_____

_____

Now, follow this recipe to grow your own crystals and answer the questions.

First, place several pieces of brick or briquettes in a container. Mix together ¼ cup salt (60 milliliters), ¼ cup laundry bluing (60 milliliters), ¼ cup water (60 milliliters), and 1 tablespoon of ammonia (15 milliliters). Pour this over the brick or briquettes and sprinkle on several drops of food coloring.

Complete the chart by filling in the date and time you started your garden and then recording when you notice the changes listed below.

	Date	**Time**
Solution poured on		
First crystals appear		
No liquid remains		
No new crystals forming		

Describe what kinds of changes you observed as your garden grew.

_____

_____

_____

Draw and color a picture of your garden on the back of this page.

Based on the crystal growth pattern you observed, how do you think you could grow bigger crystals?

_____

_____

You many want to make another garden to test your idea.

Name_____

111

In the phone book

Want to find out how many names are in your city's phone directory? You can spend the next few weeks counting. Or, conduct a sample survey and make a prediction.

To do a sample survey, select at random three full pages of names from the directory and find out how many names are on each of the pages. You can count the names individually, but that's a lot of counting. It's easier to divide the page into four equal parts, count how many names are on one-fourth of the page, and multiply by 4. Do this for each of the pages you select. Now add the totals for the three pages together and divide that number by 3 to find the average number of names on a sample page.

1. How many names are in your sample survey?

_____

2. How many pages of names are in your city's directory?

_____

3. Multiply the number of names in your sample survey by the total number of pages with names. How many names do you predict are in your local directory?

_____

The city with the most telephones is New York with 5,808,145.

Name _____

Especially for K-2

Introducing Predicting

The essence of making predictions is recognizing patterns. Help your students learn to look for patterns by setting up water bells. Fill six glass quart jars with different amounts of water so that each jar contains more water than the one before. Add a few drops of food coloring to each jar to make the water level more visible. Tell the children to listen carefully for how the sounds differ. Then strike the first three jars in order, starting with the one that is least full. Ask your students to describe what they notice about the sounds. Lead them to conclude that the greater the amount of water the higher the sound. Explain that this discovery is a pattern. Now ask the kids to use this pattern to predict whether the sound of the next bell will be higher or lower than the first three. (It will be higher because the jar is fuller.) After the children respond, strike the jar to demonstrate the concept of pattern and reinforce their confidence in using it. Continue this exercise by having the students predict the sound level of the last two bells.

EXTENDERS:

FOLLOW THE LEADER
(small groups)
Play this rhythm game with four or five children while the others are active in learning centers. First, ask the kids to stand in a circle. Then produce a simple clapping pattern for them. For example, clap twice quickly, then once slowly, then twice quickly again. Repeat your pattern several times. Now clap just part of the pattern, point to a student, and have him or her continue with what comes next. Then complete the pattern yourself. After several children have had a chance to finish the pattern, allow a student to become the leader.

OUR WEATHER CALENDAR
(whole class)
SUPPLIES: posterboard, crayons or markers, cotton balls, glue
EXPERIENCE: Help your students become aware that it's possible to forecast weather conditions because weather occurs in predictable patterns. Use the posterboard to create a large calendar. Make the spaces for each day large enough to record simple weather information. Have the kids take turns drawing and coloring bright suns, raindrops, snowflakes, or adding cottonball clouds, on the calendar. Use similar symbols to report the forecast for each day, on the chalkboard. Ask your students to compare the forecast with what they have observed.

USING THE ACTIVITIES:

On pages 114-115, you'll find activities that will help your students learn to recognize patterns and use them for predicting. After finishing each activity, the children might create predicting exercises of their own. Have them switch with a friend and figure each other's out. Individual references for the activity pages are given below. Read the worksheets before you look at the suggestions in this section.

SPACE BUGS, page 114
(whole class)
Students can do this simple fill-in-the-blank number sequence activity without much help from you. After they finish, let them color the bugs.

ON TIME, page 115
(whole class or homework)
EXPERIENCE: Give your students this activity to help them practice telling time. Explain that sometimes memories help us become aware of patterns. For example, some events happen around a certain time of day. Point to the line drawn from the clock that says 7:15 A.M. to the child getting dressed in the bedroom. Tell your students that early in the morning children usually get up and get dressed for school. Guide the kids through completing this worksheet or send it home for parent or adult involvement.
FOLLOW-UP: Show the class a large poster board clock with movable hands. Set it to a certain time and tell the children whether the time shown is "A.M." or "P.M." Give them two activities from which to choose. Ask them to predict which of these is the most likely to be done at that time of day.

Space bugs

Look at the pictures of the bugs. First, find out how the numbers are arranged. Then, use this pattern to decide which numbers are missing. Write the missing numbers. Fill-in the blank parts of each bug.

Name _____

On time

Look at the clock that says 7:15 A.M. Someone has drawn a line from it to the picture showing what would happen at that time of day. Connect each of the other clocks to the correct picture in the same way.

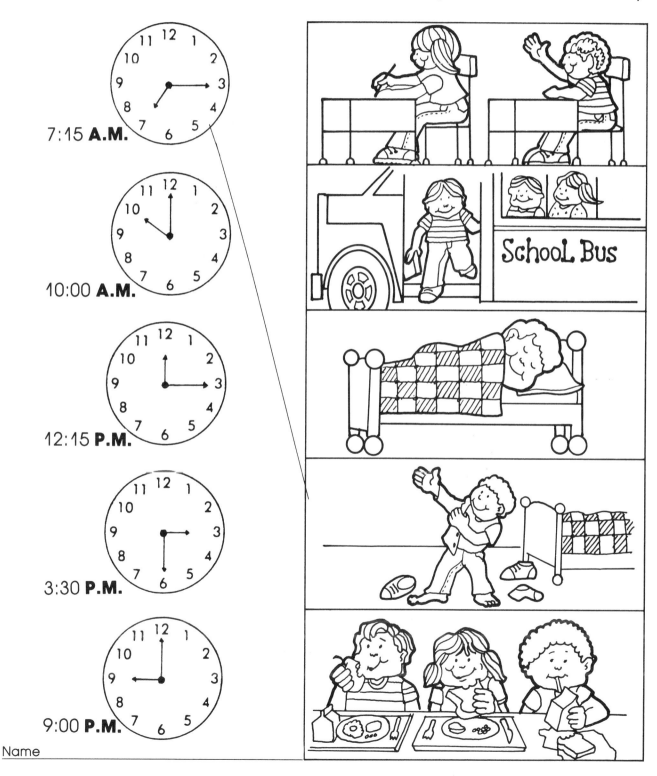

7:15 **A.M.**

10:00 **A.M.**

12:15 **P.M.**

3:30 **P.M.**

9:00 **P.M.**

Name

115

MARCH
Focusing on
Measuring

HIGHLIGHTS OF THE MONTH

3 U.S. Bureau of Forestry changed its name in 1905

After this date, the Bureau became officially known as the U.S. Forest Service. Have your students discover information about the Service. It is a branch of the Department of Agriculture which manages 190 million acres of forests in the U.S. and Puerto Rico. One of its main duties is to fight and prevent forest fires. Who is its most famous ranger? Smokey the Bear! The Forest Service is also responsible for protecting forests against disease, preserving wildlife, and supervising picnic and campgrounds. To celebrate the founding of the Forest Service, have your kids adopt a tree. Then turn to "Tree-mendous" on pages 122-123, for some tree-measuring action.

7 First sewing machine to stitch buttonholes patented by Charles Miller (U.S.) in 1854

Take a close look at your buttonholes in honor of this invention. Are they horizontal or vertical? Large or small? Ask your students what other attributes they might use to classify buttonholes. Then keep kids in stitches by giving them the activity, "So it Seams" on page 124.

7 Luther Burbank (U.S.) born in 1849

Burbank, an American naturalist, is best remembered for having developed over 800 new varieties of flowers, fruits, vegetables, and trees. To develop these new varieties, Burbank crossed two different plants by placing the pollen from one stigma of a flower to another. He usually grew thousands of plants in his effort to produce one newly improved species. (Some famous hybrids developed from Burbank's work are the Russet potato and Shasta Daisy!) Each year Santa Rosa, California, holds a festival to honor Burbank. To celebrate his contributions, plant some seeds following the directions provided by the activity "The Great Bean Race" on pages 125-126. Then measure what sprouts.

13 Uranus discovered in 1781

When Sir William Herschel (Great Britain) first spotted this planet, he thought he'd seen a comet. The planet was named Herschel in his honor, but the name was later changed to Uranus, after a greek god, to fit the names given to the other planets. Have your students discover interesting facts about Uranus (It is the third largest planet, Uranus takes 84 years to revolve around the sun, it has five moons.) Ask your students to compare the measurements of Uranus and Earth.

14 Chester Greenwood (U.S.) patented earmuffs in 1877

Your students probably wear earmuffs without appreciating how handy they are for keeping ears warm. Chester Greenwood invented earmuffs in 1873 when he was only fifteen! Winters in Farmington, Maine, where he lived, were very cold. He'd gotten a brand new pair of ice skates, but couldn't skate as long as he wanted because his ears kept getting cold. The hats he tried blew off and scarves were itchy, so Chester made two ear-sized loops out of baling wire and got his grandmother to sew pieces of fur on one side and black velvet on the other. Then his grandmother connected the fur-covered muffs to a cap. Chester's invention worked so well that other people soon wanted earmuffs too. The rest is history. Ask your students to put some earmuffs on and go outside to measure the temperature. And give them the activity, "How Cold Is It?" on page 127.

16 First liquid-fuel rocket launched in 1926

Have kids discover the history of rockets. (Rockets were used, especially in warfare throughout the last few centuries. The Chinese in the 13th century were the first to use rockets. Rockets were used during the Revolutionary War, remind students of the line in the STAR SPANGLED BANNER: "Oh the rockets' red glare!") Earlier rockets used dry powders. Robert Goddard (U.S.) was the first to use liquid fuel to propel a rocket. His invention ushered in a whole new era paving the way for the development of missiles, satellites, and the exploring of space! In Goddard's honor, have students complete the activity, "3, 2, 1, Blast Off!" on pages 36-37.

31 Daylight savings time first went into effect in 1918

Daylight savings time was an idea that Benjamin Franklin proposed! It was implemented in Great Britain during World War I, in order to save coal. Later, in 1918, it was tried in the United States. This time change is mainly popular in cities, not in rural areas. Can kids explain why? Start your students measuring time. Give them the activity "It's About Time" on page 128.

Introducing Measuring

Grades 3 and up

Start off by measuring your students heights. (You could display this information on a chart or a graph.) Height is a familiar measurement for kids. Point out that being measured is one of the first things that happens to people after birth. Measurements continue throughout life. When kids measure how big, how heavy, how warm, or how much time, they give dimensions to their world.

Once your students start to experiment, though, they need to learn to measure the way a scientist would—using the metric scale. To help kids relate commonly-used metric measurements to familiar English ones, provide these examples:

Draw pictures of the following items on a board or poster. Label with these measurements: 1 liter, 1 quart, 1 meter, 1 yard, 1 kilogram, and 1 pound

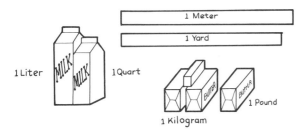

The best way for kids to learn metric measurements is to measure. Making kites gives them the perfect opportunity to do this—and have fun—in this windy month. Each child will need a large plastic trash bag; two 3-millimeter (1/8-inch) wooden dowels, 53 centimeters (21¼ inches) long; the cardboard tube from a toilet-paper roll; a stick that fits through the tube; and at least 20 meters (65½ feet) of monofilament fishing line. You'll also need to supply transparent tape, package-sealing tape, hole punches, scissors, felt-tip markers, and meter sticks. Guide students step by step through the directions found on pages 120-121 of Let's Go Fly a Kite.

Once your students have finished building their kites, they will want to try flying them. Check weather reports for wind speed (something else to measure in March) and have the kids make their test flights when winds are light to moderate. Choose an open area away from trees or overhead wires that could be a source of danger. To unwind their flying line, the children should put sticks through the tubes and hold onto both ends. Ask your students to write about their kite-flying experience. Have them share their tips for successful flights. Also, encourage the kids to find out about the history of kites. For example, Benjamin Franklin, who in the 1700s did a kite-flying experiment (although it was foolishly dangerous) to prove that lightning was a form of electricity. Find out about the use and design of kites in other cultures.

EXTENDERS:

PLANT PETS
(whole class)
SUPPLIES: a piece of string for each child
EXPERIENCE: Keep your students measuring this month by having them track the growth of two or three pet plants. First, ask students to select sprouts in the school yard and give them pet names. Show the kids how to use a string to measure the height of their plants and tell them to do this every day. Have the children make a chart with a column for each pet plant and record the measurements daily in the correct column. (You can also use the growth of leaves, instead of plants, for this activity.)

FILL IT UP
(center)
SUPPLIES: plastic measuring cup, water, five different-sized containers
EXPERIENCE: Set up a measuring center by a sink or a wading pool. Challenge your students to find out how many liters of water it takes to fill each of the five containers.

A MEASURED EVENT
(whole class)
SUPPLIES: metric tape measure, timer
EXPERIENCE: Are track and field events in the news? Hold a mini-field day of your own. Kids can measure distances for races and time the events.

118

USING THE ACTIVITIES:

To complete the activities, which appear on pages 122-128, your students need to do such tasks as recording temperatures and averaging heights. Whether the kids are required to compute degrees, hours, or centimeters, they have a chance to practice the process skill of measuring. After your students have mastered the tasks in the activities, you may want to have them share basic ways of "finding out how much" with children from other classes. Following the activity titles in this section, are individual page numbers for the worksheets. Refer to them before you read the instructions given here.

TREE-MENDOUS, pages 122-123
(homework)
EXPERIENCE: How much do branches grow each year? Give your students this take-home activity so they can measure and find out. Allow time in class for them to share their results. You may also want to have the kids use their statistics to compute average branch growth for this year and last year.
FOLLOW-UP: If you have large trees on your school grounds, take the class outside. Ask each student to look for a tree which seems about the same diameter as the student. Then have each student measure his or her waist and the tree's circumference to see how similar they are in size.

SO IT SEAMS, page 124
(center)
SUPPLIES: an old, long-sleeved shirt, a 1-meter (3 ⅓-foot) piece of string, a meter stick
EXPERIENCE: Help your students learn how to take clothing measurements with this practical activity. Be sure the kids understand where the seams are to be measured on the shirt. You may also want to have the children measure the size of the buttonholes, the distance between the buttonholes, and the length of the shirt from the base of the collar to the bottom of the shirttail.

THE GREAT BEAN RACE*
pages 125-126
(whole class or small groups)
SUPPLIES: a styrofoam cup and six seeds for each child, shallow boxes, plastic trash bags, firm plastic spoons, fine gravel, potting soil, clear plastic wrap, water

*Challenging activity

EXPERIENCE: Use the garbage bags to line the boxes and put them in a warm place away from drafts and direct sunlight. After the children plant their seeds, have them write their names on strips of masking tape and stick the labels on the sides of their potting cups. Ask the students to place the cups in one of the boxes to prevent water from spilling or leaking on furniture. Also, grow a control plant and assign someone to measure and record its results on the class chart for comparison. At the end of the week, allow time to share results. How many people had beans taller than the control? Whose beans were the tallest each day? You may want to award a certificate to daily winners and/or to the grand champion. Students can also work on this activity in small groups.

HOW COLD IS IT?, page 127
(small groups)
SUPPLIES: a Celsius indoor/outdoor thermometer for each group
EXPERIENCE: Prepare your students for this activity by teaching them how to read thermometers. They should hold the thermometer by the supporting frame so the heat from their fingers won't affect the results. Have them find the highest and lowest numbers on the scales and figure out how many degrees each small line represents. Allow time for the groups to share their results. Students may also plan and carry out an experiment to test how wind affects the temperature.

IT'S ABOUT TIME, page 128
(pairs)
SUPPLIES: gallon-size plastic milk jugs
EXPERIENCE: First, everyone in the class should find a partner. One child should perform the tasks in the activity, while the other child times him or her. Have the class discuss the results.
FOLLOW-UP: Ask the kids to put their heads down on their desks, close their eyes, and be absolutely quiet for one minute. Tell them that as soon as they think a minute has passed, they should lift up their heads. Watch the clock, and each time a student signals that a minute is up, record the actual number of seconds that has passed. How many students were able to judge one minute exactly? How many were close? Or, set up a simple obstacle course. Post a chart and have each student record his or her time on it. Challenge the kids to improve their times.

Let's go fly a kite!

1. Cut a 38-centimeter (15-inch) square from the trash bag.

2. Fold the square in half diagonally. Then unfold it and draw a line on the crease. Following diagram 1, make a mark 15 centimeters (6 inches) from the top end of the center line and fold down the top corner as shown. Unfold the corner and draw a line on the new crease. On this cross line, mark dots A and B, each 13 millimeters (½ inch) from the center line as shown in diagram 2. Make dots C and D the same way. Center a square piece of transparent tape over each dot and punch a hole through it.

3. Make the spar. Place a dowel across the center line, going from the tip of one wing to the other. Use tape to attach the spar at the wing tips and trim tape as shown in diagram 3.

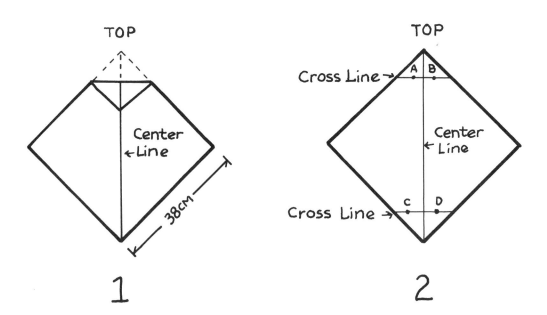

4. Make the spine. Position the remaining dowel from the top to the bottom of the kite, crossing underneath the spar. Tape the spine at the top (using the same method as for the spar) and at the point where the spar and the spine cross, as shown in diagram 4. (Make sure the spine is taped securely so it won't move and cause the kite to loop in flight.)

5. Make the bridle. Cut a 73 centimeter (29 inch) piece of the fishing line. With the spine facing you, thread one end of the line through hole B, around the back, and up through hole A. Tie the line over the spine. Thread the opposite line through the bottom set of holes and tie it the same way.

6. Make the streamers. From the trash bag, cut two plastic strips each about 2½ centimeters (1 inch) wide and 38 centimeters (15 inches) long. Tape these streamers to the wing tips as shown in diagram 5.

Name _____

7. Make the tail. Cut a plastic strip 5 centimeters (2 inches) wide and 110 centimeters (44 inches) long. Following diagram 5, use packaging tape to attach these paper cross pieces to the tail, spacing them about 10 centimeters (4 inches) apart. Tape the tail to the bottom of the kite as shown.

8. Make the flying line. Tape one end of the remaining monofilament line to the cardboard tube and then wind on the line. Pull the bridle knots tight. Following diagram 5, tie the free end of the flying line to the midpoint of the bridle.

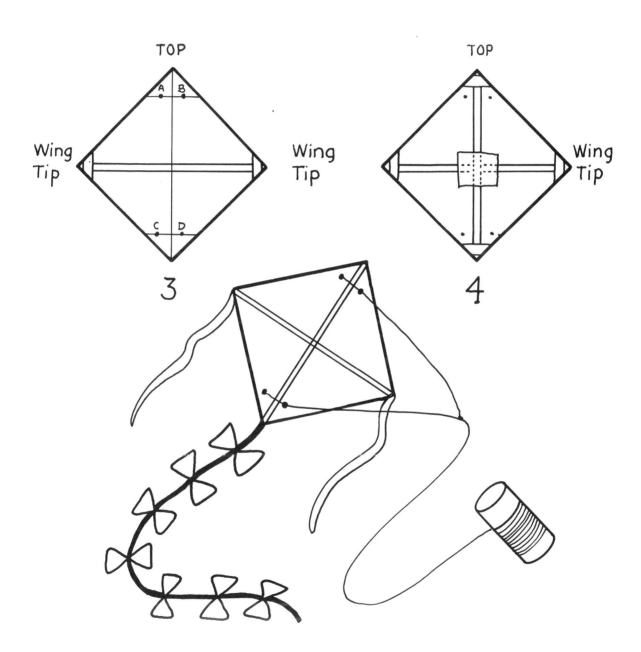

Tree-mendous

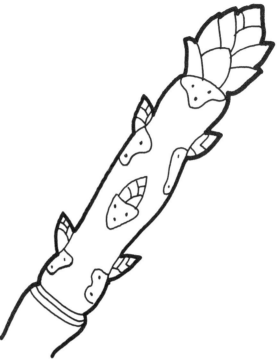

When you grow taller, your arms grow longer. That's the way a tree grows, too. As it stretches toward the sky, each of the tree's branches becomes a little longer. How much does a branch grow in a year? Does every branch on a tree grow the same amount? Here's how to find out. You'll need a pencil or pen, a piece of string, and a centimeter ruler. Take these supplies outside and find a tree that has branches with tips you can reach. Choose one branch to look for and examine the terminal bud and the annual rings (see diagram).

Next, measure from the top of the annual rings to the tip of the terminal bud. That's how much the branch grew this year. Then look farther down the branch for another set of rings. Those are last year's annual rings. Measure the distance between the two sets of rings. That is how much the branch grew last year.

Measure this year's and last year's growth on five different branches. Record this growth information on the chart. Then answer the questions.

Branch	Centimeters Grew This Year	Centimeters Grew Last Year
1		
2		
3		
4		
5		

Name _____

1. Do all the branches on a tree grow the same amount in a year?

☐ Yes ☐ No

Does a branch grow the same amount each year? _____

2. What are some variables that could affect how much a branch grows?

Mystery Trees

Each of the scrambled words below is the name of a mystery tree. First, unscramble the names, then see if you can find them in the puzzle. Look up and down, across, and diagonally. Circle each name.

EAMLP _____   NIPE _____   SAH _____

WDEODOR _____   KOA _____   MAPL _____

EYSCRAMO _____   LIWLOW _____   REDAC _____

MEL _____   HRCIB _____   TNLUAW _____

A	O	I	P	W	I	L	L	O	W
B	S	Y	C	A	M	O	R	E	U
I	E	H	E	L	M	A	P	L	E
R	L	B	D	N	P	I	N	E	T
C	M	D	A	U	O	A	K	G	C
H	E	V	R	T	U	I	L	H	M
R	E	D	W	O	O	D	D	M	X

Name _____

So it seams

Pretend you're a tailor about to make a new shirt for the President of the United States. The President is not available, so you can't take measurements. But you have a favorite shirt to measure instead.

Start by checking the neck-to-shoulder seam. Lay the shirt on a flat surface and straighten the material, making sure all of the seam is showing. Then match one end of the string to the beginning of the seam. With your left hand, hold this end down so it stays in place as you stretch the string along the seam with your right hand. When you get to the end of the seam, pinch the string. (Be sure the string is pulled tight.) Then, still pinching the string, lay it along a meter stick. Measure up to the pinched spot. Use this same method for all the other seams. Write each measurement on the line provided for it below.

Neck seam _____   Shoulder-to-wrist seam _____

Neck-to-shoulder seam _____   Underarm seam _____

Shoulder-to-shoulder seam _____

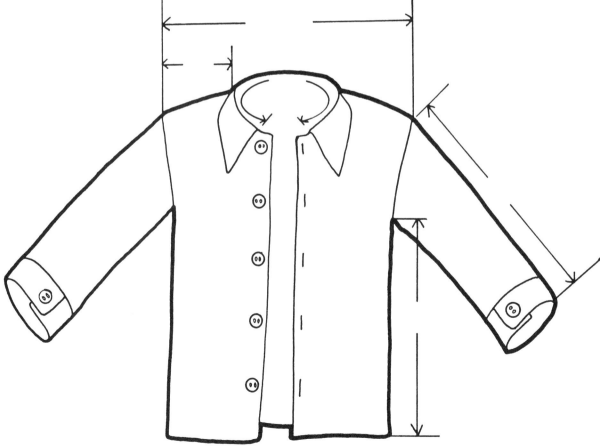

Name _____

The great bean race

Your class is having a race to see who can grow the tallest bean plants. To enter the race, follow the directions for starting your sprouts. Grow all your plants, except one, under the same conditions set for the others. Five days later, at the end of the race, look at the plant-height averages displayed on the class chart to see who won.

To start your sprouts, soak six bean seeds in water overnight. Use a pencil with a sharp point to poke three small holes in the bottom of a plastic-foam cup. Pour 30 milliliters (two tablespoons) of gravel into the cup. Fill the rest of the cup with potting soil. Bury the soaked bean seeds just below the surface. Cover the cup with plastic wrap and place it on the drainage tray prepared by your teacher. Sprinkle two tablespoons of water on the soil. While your seeds are growing, water them this way every other day. As soon as you see a sprout, remove the plastic wrap.

Name _____

Up to this point, all the bean plants have been grown under the same conditions. The variables that have been controlled are: amount of soil, size of pot, number of plants, exposure to sunlight, and amount of water. Now decide how you will change one of these variables. For example you can either expose your plants to full sun, give them three tablespoons of water daily, or choose your own original test variable.

What are you going to change? _____

_____

On the first day of the race, put your change into effect, but be sure to control all the other variables as before.

Every day of the contest, measure each of your bean plants. To do this, stretch a string along the length of the plant, then pinch the string so it shows the height of the plant. Carefully holding the string at this point, lay it alongside a centimeter ruler and measure up to the pinched point. Record the measurements for each day on the chart below. (If a sprout is not yet visible, put a zero for its height.) Add these measurements to get your total, then record it on the chart. Divide the total by 6 (the number of plants) to get your average daily plant height. Record this number both on your chart and on the class chart.

Bean Plant	Day 1	Day 2	Day 3	Day 4	Day 5
1					
2					
3					
4					
5					
6					
Total					
Average					

Name _____

126

How cold is it?

The weather report tells what the temperature is. But, is the air really that temperature everywhere? Go to each of the places listed on the chart. Wait five minutes to give the thermometer time to adjust to any change. Then check and record the temperature.

Location   **Temperature in Degrees Celsius**

In the shade

In full sun

Close to a building

In an open area

1. Where was the temperature the warmest?

_____

2. Where was it the coldest?

_____

3. How could you test if wind affects the temperature?

_____

_____

Name _____

It's about time

Use a clock to time each pair of events and circle the one that takes longer.

1. Filling a plastic gallon milk jug

   Emptying the same milk jug

2. Walking across the length of a room

   Hopping across the same room

3. Putting on a jacket and zipping or buttoning it

   Taking off the same jacket

4. Putting on a sock and a shoe

   Taking off the same sock and shoe

Circle the unit of time that would most likely be used to answer each of these questions.

1. How long is it until the Fourth of July?   Weeks   Months

2. How long do you spend taking a bath?   Seconds   Minutes

3. How long is it until Saturday?   Hours   Days

4. How long does it take to bake a cake?   Seconds   Minutes

5. How old is your dad, or mom, brother or sister?   Months   Years

6. How long does it take to blow out the candles on your birthday cake?   Seconds   Minutes

Name _____

Especially for K-2
Introducing Measuring

Help your students develop an awareness of the concept of measuring with a very personal unit—their hands. Demonstrate how to measure a desk top by placing the side of each hand against the edge of a desk. Start with your right hand at one end of the edge and your left hand in front of your right, just barely touching it. Say "one, two," and put your right hand in front of your left for "three." Then move your left hand ahead of your right for "four." Continue until you've crossed the top of the desk. You may want to have the kids round to the nearest whole hand or to say one half if there's only room for part of a hand at the opposite side.

Once your students have gotten the idea, have them fill out a chart with their own personal measurements. For younger children, show a picture as well as the name of the object to be measured. Include a chair (height from the floor to the top of the back or width of the seat), a desk (height from the floor to the desk top), and a book (length and width). For small objects, such as a pencil, have the kids measure using their right and left index fingers. For very large things, such as the width and length of the room, have them measure by stepping the distance with their feet—heel to toe.

Let kids share their results for such items as a chair. Ask why the resulting measurements are so different, and what will happen to these personal measuring scales as the children grow older.

EXTENDERS:

HOW BIG WAS IT?
(whole class)
SUPPLIES: a ball of string, pictures of dinosaurs
EXPERIENCE: Kids know that dinosaurs were big, but the concept of hugeness needs developing. Find out the length of several of these prehistoric giants. An Apatosaurus averaged 21 meters (70 feet). The Tyrannosaurus was about 15 meters (50 feet). Choose one of the dinosaurs and measure a piece of string to match the animal's size. Show the class pictures, tell a few facts about the dinosaurs, and compare their lengths. Then focus on the dinosaur of your choice and discuss what scientists say about its habits. Go outside to stretch out the string and see how big this beast really was. You may want to have your students line up along the string, or even lie down head to foot, to experience how many children it would take to equal one of these giants.

BIG/LITTLE HUNT
(whole class)
Take advantage of the milder weather by going outside to develop this measuring concept. Have everyone sit in a circle. Ask the children to be quiet for one minute and really look at everything around them. Then have them tell you the biggest or the smallest thing they see. Tell the kids to join hands and circle something, a tree or even the school sign, to see how many children fit around it. What else can you measure this way? Ask kids how big they can stretch and how small they can make themselves. Have the class join hands and stretch into the biggest circle they can make. Then let them squeeze together into the smallest circle.

USING THE ACTIVITIES:

Teaching concepts such as big and small or more and less to primary-grade children can be a challenging task. The activities that appear on pages 131-132, focus on the process skill of measuring and make learning these concepts easy and enjoyable for your students. After kids finish the activities, encourage them to continue using the concepts in their daily lives. You might also want to add words such as *tiny* and *huge* to create a scale the children can understand. In this section, you'll find helpful suggestions on ways to present these activities. Be sure to look at the worksheets as you read these comments.

HOW BIG IS IT, page 131
(whole class)
Give this activity to your students so they can practice three skills: sequencing as they connect the dots, observing as they

identify the frog, and measuring as they compare the frog's size to their own. Verbally reinforce each skill used. When the kids finish, have them draw a life-sized picture of a frog. Give each child a sheet of paper with two marks 7½ centimeters (3 inches) apart on it. Tell the kids to draw their frogs from one mark to the other.

THE CONTEST, page 132
(whole class)
Prepare your students for this activity by explaining that one way of measuring is to answer "how much of something there is."

Cut out felt shapes, such as circles, and display these in sets on a flannelboard. Ask the kids to tell you which set has more. Switch the number of shapes in the sets and ask again. Or, use tape or chalk to mark two circles on the floor. Call on a different number of students to stand in each circle. Help the kids to understand the different ways to look at measuring quantities by asking which group has more, which group is bigger, and which group is fuller. Regroup several times. You may also want to ask which group has fewer, is smaller, and is less full. Next, give students the activity. Take time to discuss their choices afterwards.

How big is it?

Start at number 1. Connect the dots to see an animal. Answer the questions about it.

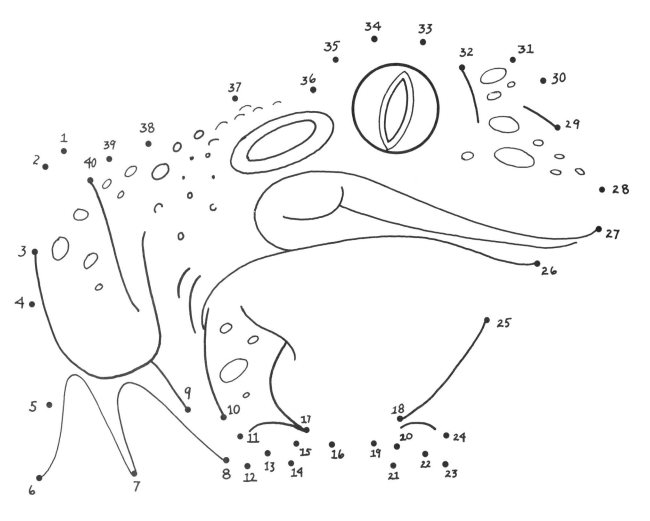

1. What is this animal?   ☐ Rabbit   ☐ Elephant   ☐ Frog   ☐ Giraffe

2. Is it big or small? _____

3. Is it bigger or smaller than you are? _____

Name _____

The contest

Sarah and Ben had a contest. They wanted to see who could find the most of each of these things. The chart below tells what the children collected. For each type of thing, circle the largest group to show who has more.

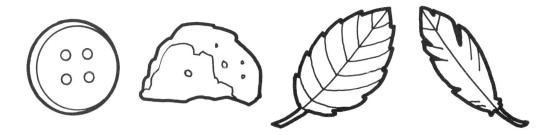

Sarah's things	**Ben's things**

The person with the most circles wins. Who won—Sarah or Ben?

_____

APRIL
Focusing on
Designing an Experiment

2 Charles Martin Hall (U.S.) patented a method for producing aluminum commercially in 1889

Your students may find it hard to believe that aluminum was once so difficult to separate from aluminum ore that it was both rare and valuable. In fact, the very top of the Washington Monument in Washington, D.C. is a pyramid of pure aluminum. Hall changed this when he found that aluminum could be extracted inexpensively using electrolysis. Have your students read to find out how electrolysis works. Then ask them to list what variables Hall probably had to control while he was experimenting with this process. (Hall dissolved alumina, aluminum ore, in a bath of cryolite and passed an electric current through the solution. So he probably had to control the temperature of the solution, the amount of dissolved alumina, the amount of cryolite, and the voltage among other things.)

6 Robert Peary (U.S.) discovered the North Pole in 1909

Did Peary make it on his first try? Was it an easy trip? Did he arrive alone? Have your students research to discover the details of this famous expedition. (He made several unsuccessful attempts before reaching the Pole. The successful expedition encountered several close calls, including having to cut ice rafts to ferry sleds, dogs, and men across open water. He arrived with his Black aide, Matthew Henson, and four Eskimos.) While kids are appreciating this cold trip, give them the activity "The Ice Test" on page 137.

10 Dr. Arnold M. Collins (U.S.) first commercially manufactured neoprene, synthetic rubber, in 1930

Why was the discovery of neoprene important? (It was found that natural rubber could be harmed by sunlight, air, gas, and high temperature, therefore a substitute had to be found.) Neoprene is now used in making rubber hoses, insulation, cables, and many types of sportswear. Display samples of neoprene and real rubber for kids to compare in honor of this event. Then stretch kids' thinking powers

with the activity "That's Stretching It" on page 139.

12 The Big Wind blew in 1934

The highest velocity wind ever recorded on Earth was observed on top of Mount Washington, New Hampshire. How windy was it? Have your students check in the *Guinness Book of World Records* to find out. (The wind was blowing at 231 mph/372 kph.) Check the weather report to record your local wind speed today. Then ask your kids to do "The Big Blow" on page 140.

12 Yuri Gagarin (U.S.S.R.) became the first man in space in 1961

This Russian air force pilot traveled at a speed of 17000 mph/ 24000 kph. The trip lasted 108-minutes, and the highest point reached was 203 mi/327 km above Earth. The voyage was made aboard *Vostok I*. Have your students research the experiments that were done to make manned spaceflight possible. (See also "3, 2, 1, Blast Off" on pages 36-37.)

14 Nimbus II satellite provided the first successful view of Earth's atmosphere in 1969

The Nimbus II was a type of weather satillite which relayed data to Earth about atmospheric conditions. Based on this information weather reports could be developed. Celebrate this event by watching a satellite's view of changing cloud patterns on a television weather report. (See also "Satellite Sort" on pages 32-33.)

Arbor Day first observed in 1872

Who is the father of Arbor Day? Julius Sterling Morton (U.S.). Morton intended the day as a holiday set aside for the planting of trees. Arbor Day occurs on different dates in different parts of the country and celebrates the future through the planting of seeds and seedlings. In some states, schools close so that children can participate in Arbor Day festivals. Though the custom originated in the United States, it has become popular in other countries as well. In fact now International Arbor Day is celebrated in December, see page 70. To celebrate, give your students the activity "Just Leafy" on page 138.

Introducing Designing an Experiment

Grades 3 and up

Your students are now ready to design their own experiments. To do this, they need to learn how to state a hypothesis and write an investigation plan. Both of these tasks require that kids apply the process skills they've learned: observing, controlling variables, and inferring.

Explain that the first step in setting up an experiment is to identify all the variables. Remind students that variables are things that can change and affect the outcome of an experiment. As an example, write a starting question on the board. "How does being wet, rather than dry, affect seeds' sprouting?" Give each child several different kinds of seeds (such as dried beans, sunflower seeds, and popcorn kernels). Ask the kids to observe their seeds for all the variables that could affect the results of the experiment and tell you what they discover. Write "Object Variables" as a heading on the chalkboard and list suggestions under this. The variables should include: type of plant seed, size of seed, and thickness of seed coat.

Then write a second heading, "Environmental Variables," and explain that these are conditions which could affect the results. You may want to tell students that in an experiment they should always consider these environmental factors: air temperature, exposure to sunlight, humidity, and air movement. The students may suggest more variables for each of these lists. The important thing for them to remember is that all the variables except the one being tested in an experiment need to be controlled.

Tell the kids that the second step is picking the one variable that will be tested. Explain that this variable is called the *manipulated variable* because it is the one being changed in some specific way. Ask students to look back at the question you wrote on the board and identify what factor will be tested. Lead them to conclude that it's whether or not moisture is present. Write "the manipulated variable is water."

Explain that as part of this step in designing an experiment, it's necessary to decide what kind of results to look for. This is a variable, too. It's called the *responding variable*. Ask your students to look at the starting question again to identify what the responding variable will be for this experiment. Lead them to conclude it's the sprouting of the seeds'. Write "the responding variable is sprouting " on the chalkboard.

Now your students are ready to use the information they worked out to construct a hypothesis. Tell them that a *hypothesis* is a guess about the relationship between the manipulated and responding variables. The hypothesis can be based on a hunch or facts. You need to use words, such as increase and decrease, or faster and slower, to predict what effect changing the manipulated variable will have on the responding variable. Write this hypothesis on the chalkboard as an example: "As the wetness of the seeds increases, the rate at which they sprout will also increase."

For practice, work together to state other hypotheses, using "seeds' sprouting" as the responding variable, but changing the manipulated variable to "exposure to sunlight," then to "type of plant seed," and finally to "temperature." The hypotheses are: "As the exposure to sunlight increases, the time it takes for the seeds to sprout decreases."

"Some varieties of seeds sprout faster than others."

"As the temperature decreases, the number of seeds that will sprout also decreases."

Your students will undoubtedly think of others. Just check for a direct relationship between the two key variables.

Finally, tell your students that to develop an investigative plan, they need to answer these three questions:
1. In what way will you change the manipulated variable?
2. In what way will you measure the responding variable?

3. What variables will you control?

Ask your students to answer these questions for the sample hypothesis about the effect of water on seeds' sprouting. An answer for the first question is to soak the seeds for different amounts of time, such as 10 minutes, 20 minutes, 30 minutes, and so forth. The answer to the second question is the number of days it takes the seeds to sprout. The answer to the third is all the object and environmental variables that were listed during the "get ready" steps, other than the manipulated and responding variables.

EXTENDERS:

Designing an experiment is much like solving a puzzle. Help your students become proficient in using this important problem-solving tool and to develop a feeling that designing experiments is fun, with these activities.

SPRINGTIME FANCIES
(whole class)
Take advantage of the many changes kids observe in the spring to have them practice identifying variables and formulating hypotheses. For example, one day when the trees first begin to leaf out, write on the chalkboard: "Do all the leaves on a tree unfold at the same rate?" Challenge your students to come up with all the possible variables that could affect an investigation of this question. Or, list the following sets of springtime manipulating and responding variables: rain/erosion, length of days/plant growth, number of flowers/bee activity. Have the kids construct a hypotheses for each set.

A HEARTY RATING
(whole class)
After recess, write this question on the board: "Does exercise affect your heart rate?" Ask your students to come up with a manipulating and a responding variable for an experiment designed to answer this question.

USING THE ACTIVITIES:

The activities on pages 137-140 help children to understand how to design an experiment. Testing some of the hypotheses at home or at a science center encourages

*Challenging activity

increased interest and provides needed practical experience. Individual references for the worksheets are given following the activity titles here. Be sure to look at these before you read the helpful hints in this section.

THE ICE TEST, page 137
(whole class)
Give your students this activity to help them focus on the variables in an experiment and practice following the step-by-step procedure scientists use to design one. Before the kids begin, make sure they really understand the meaning of the terms *object variable*, *environmental variable*, *manipulated variable*, and *responding variable*. Then have the children make a list of all the variables that could affect the melting rate of the ice. Let the kids classify these as object or environmental variables and answer the questions to design the experiment.

JUST LEAFY, page 138
(whole class)
This activity, presents your students with valuable practice in constructing hypotheses. Allow time to discuss kids' responses. Be sure to point out to the children that, as they've just seen, a scientific investigation may be designed in more than one way. Expand this activity by having students think of other variables and construct hypotheses for these.

THAT'S STRETCHING IT, page 139
(whole class)
Let your students study good experimental design by reading the model experiment. As they analyze this one to find key points and answer the questions, they have the chance to apply what they've learned about designing an experiment. Expand the activity by selecting other experiments from your science text. For each of these, ask your students to answer the same questions.

THE BIG BLOW, page 140*
(whole class)
Challenge your students with this activity, which requires them to work through the getting-ready steps and plan the design for an experiment. The hypothesis in this activity is a good one to test at a science center. Supply materials and have the kids perform the experiment that they design. Allow time for them to share results.

136

The ice test

What if you wanted to find out what determines how quickly ice melts?

1. What are some variables that might affect the melting rate?

Object Variables	Environmental Variables
_____	_____
_____	_____
_____	_____
_____	_____

2. Which variable is the manipulating variable?

_____

3. What is the responding variable? _____

4. How would you measure the responding variable?

_____

_____

_____

_____

Name _____

Just leafy

You may have noticed that trees and bushes in some parts of your backyard have leaves while the same type of plants in other sections are bare. You have probably wondered what factors might affect the rate at which a plant leafs out in the spring. These are the variables you listed as possibilities: amount of direct sunlight the plant receives, amount of water the plant gets, and size of the plant.

Construct a hypothesis for each of these variables.

1. Amount of direct sunlight

_____

_____

_____

2. Amount of water

_____

_____

_____

3. Size of plant

_____

_____

_____

Any hypothesis is just a guess, of course, until an experiment is conducted to test it.

Name _____

138

That's stretching it

Read about this investigation and answer the questions.

Scientists performed an experiment to see how temperature affects the length a rubber band will stretch. The scientists selected four rubber bands exactly the same length and thickness and hung each one from a nail attached to a wooden support. A paper clip was bent to form a hook and looped over the bottom of the first rubber band. Next, a one-gram nut was hung on the hook. After all the rubber bands were set up this way, the scientists measured the length of each one. They then placed the rubber bands in a heat-controlled environment. Tests were done at 80° F (27° C), 90° F (32° C), 100° F (38° C), and 110° F (43° C). After that, the rubber bands were measured again.

1. What was the manipulated variable?

_____

_____

2. In what way was the manipulated variable changed?

_____

_____

_____

3. What was the responding variable?

_____

_____

_____

4. How was the responding variable measured?

_____

_____

_____

Name _____

The big blow

Answer the questions to design an experiment testing this hypothesis: "The faster the air moves, the faster water evaporates."

1. What variable will you need to manipulate?

_____

2. In what way will you change the manipulated variable?

_____

_____

_____

_____

3. How will you measure the responding variable?

_____

_____

_____

_____

_____

_____

_____

4. What variables will you need to control?

_____

_____

_____

_____

_____

_____

Name _____

Especially for K-2

Shape/Space Relationships

Your young students aren't yet ready for the level of abstract thinking required to design an experiment. However, they can begin thinking about shape and space relationships. Children can become aware of whether or not shapes have symmetry, that is, how shapes are related to each other in an orderly way. Kids can learn to recognize shapes—circles, triangles, squares and rectangles—even when they are part of an entirely different shape. This abstract processing can broaden the kinds of observations children make. It can help them make choices about attributes as they classify objects and living things. Most importantly, it can help them develop an awareness of spatial relationships — whether things are to the right or to the left.

To get started, show your students a circle. Ask them to find all the circles in your room. Help them see shapes within shapes by explaining that a circle can be found in an object such as a glass or a doorknob. Then point to some examples. Repeat this activity using a square and a triangle. Or, have your students look at magazine pictures and ask them to draw around shapes with a marker. These pictures can be displayed under the heading, "Look What Shapes I Found!" If the weather is nice, go outside to look for basic shapes in nature.

After students get used to looking for shapes, discuss the concept of symmetry. The most common kind of symmetry found in nature is bilateral, meaning that a line can be drawn to divide the shape into two matching halves. Have your students fold a circle to see that the two sides match exactly. Point out that this shows that the circle can be divided into two equal halves. Repeat this activity using both a square and an equilateral triangle. Then show the children pictures of objects and living things. Ask the kids to point out where a line can be drawn to divide each of these into two equal parts. Also ask them to think about how their own bodies have this kind of symmetry—matching right and left sides. Follow up by having your students do the activity "My Other Half" on page 143.

Next, talk about where shapes are. Walk to one side of the classroom. Hold up a circle and ask if the shape is on their right or left. Stick a brightly colored dot on each child's right hand to help distinguish between right and left. Repeat the activity with other shapes and objects. Continue by showing the shape or object moving. Ask your students to tell you if the object has moved to the left or the right. Give your students the activity "Where Is It Going?" on page 144.

EXTENDERS:

HOW LONG IS IT?
(whole class)
SUPPLIES: two pipe cleaners for each child
EXPERIENCE: A difficult but important shape/space concept is an understanding that changing an object's shape does not change its length. Give each child two pipe cleaners. Have the kids place one next to the other to see that the pipe cleaners are exactly the same length. Tell the children to bend one of the pipe cleaners in some way. Ask which pipe cleaner is now longer. The correct response is that both are still equal, only the shape has changed. Repeat this activity several times, having the kids re-shape one or the other of the pipe cleaners. Finally, show them two pictures of a snake—one stretched out and the other coiled up. Explain that these pictures are of the same snake. Ask if the snake has gotten shorter. When children are able to comprehend length, they will see that the snake's size has remained the same.

HOW MUCH IS THERE?
(whole class)
SUPPLIES: modeling clay
EXPERIENCE: This activity gives kids an opportunity to develop their ability to comprehend volume. Give each child two small, identical balls of modeling clay. First, let them examine the balls to observe that they are the same size. Then tell them to flatten one ball and ask which ball has more clay. The flattened clay will appear bigger but only the shape, not the actual amount of clay, has changed. Next, tell the children

to divide one ball into two equal parts. Then ask which has more clay. Again, they should understand that this shape manipulation doesn't change the volume. Show the class a tall narrow glass and a large shallow bowl. Fill the tall narrow container half full. Then pour the water into the large shallow container. Ask your students if there is less water than before. They should be able to tell you that the amount is the same; only the shape of the water has changed.

USING THE ACTIVITIES:

With activity pages 143-144, your students can apply what they know about space/shape relationships. You might also want the kids to look at home for examples of the concepts presented in these activities. Individual page references are given here to make it easy for you to find the worksheets. Be sure to look them over before you read the comments provided here.

MY OTHER HALF, page 143
(whole class)
After introducing the concept of symmetry, give your students this activity to reinforce what they've learned. You might divide a class of very young students into small groups and guide each group through the activity while the rest of the class is busy at learning centers.

WHERE IS IT GOING?, page 144
(whole class)
Prepare your students for this activity by helping them identify clues that show in what direction something is moving. Explain that while some things do back up, most move in the direction the head or front end is pointed. Tell the children that the wake behind the boat is a clue that it is moving forward. Ask the kids which clue helps show what direction the child is traveling. (There are tracks visible behind the boy, but not in front of him.) Allow time for students to think through this activity on their own. Then go over it with them. Let them color the pictures when they finish.

My other half

Draw a line to divide each of these things into two equal parts.

1.

2.

3.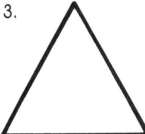

4.

5.

6.

Draw the missing half of each thing shown below.

Name _____

Where is it going?

For each picture, circle the arrow that shows which direction the thing in the picture is moving.

1.

2.

3.

4.

5.

6.

7.

8.

Name _____

4 Message sent using invisible ink in 1776

To aid the cause of the American Revolution, Silas Deane (U.S.) went to France with a letter for John Jay (U.S.). The message in this letter was interlined with a secret message about purchasing military supplies. The invisible words were written in tannic acid. To decode the message, Jay sprayed the letter with ferrous sulfate. A chemical change caused the letters to become dark and visible. Kids love secret messages. Your students will have a chance to write some as they do the activity "Now You See It—Now You Don't" on page 149.

5 Alan B. Shepard, Jr. became the first U.S. astronaut in space in 1961

Have kids read and report about the history of the space program in honor of this event. See also "3, 2, 1, Blast Off!" on pages 36-37.

6 John Gorrie (U.S.) patented the mechanical refrigerator in 1851

Collect advertisements about different brands and models of refrigerators. Display these at your science center and ask students to use at least three categories to classify the refrigerators. Kids may be surprised to discover what types of features are available in different models. Have kids practice their communication skills by writing a recipe for a treat that needs to be chilled. Then start students thinking about cold oxperiments. Give them the activity "Under-Cover Operation" on page 153.

7 Beaufort Scale created in 1805

Sir Francis Beaufort (England), a naval officer, devised this wind-force indicator. The Beaufort scale is based entirely on what can be observed. Celebrate this event and start kids observing Nature's clues to how hard the wind is blowing. Turn to the activity "What's Blowing?" on page 154.

18 In 1980, Mount Saint Helens had its first major eruption since 1857

This volcanic eruption had been successfully predicted. What pat-

MAY

Reviewing all the Process Skills

tern did scientists observe that let them predict it in time to warn people (seismic tremors, smoke, a bulge on the mountain)? To observe what happens when a volcano erupts, have your students build a volcano out of modeling clay. Tell them to put one tablespoon of baking soda into the central vent. Then have them pour in one tablespoon of vinegar. Add red food coloring for an even more realistic eruption!

27 Richard Gurley Drew (U.S.) patented masking tape in 1930
Your students will get stuck on this activity. Turn to ''Stuck on Art'' on page 152.

All Month
Many young animals are being born. Your students can bring in gelatinous amphibian eggs or tadpoles. Set up an aquarium so everyone can watch the tadpoles change into frogs, toads, or salamanders. Be sure to use pond water. Add some water plants, such as duckweed, for the tadpoles to eat. Or, boil a lettuce leaf and drop tiny bits of it into the water to feed your guests. Change the water often and keep the tadpoles out of direct sunlight. Once they're mature, return the animals to their natural habitat. For more resources, turn to the activity ''That's Frog-tastic!'' on pages 150-151.

146

Review Activities

Grades 3 and up

As the school year nears an end, this month's activities provide practice and reinforce concepts using the basic science process skills. There are also additional opportunities to work through designing an experiment.

The natural curiosity of your students will lead them to plenty of opportunities to investigate and discover, as they charge into summer— and that's great! After all, the goal of teaching kids these process skills is to provide a set of tools for exploring the world and discovering answers on their own.

EXTENDERS:

IN THE SPRINGTIME
(whole class)
Spring is in the air and a sense of newness accompanies this season. Bring in a variety of blooming flowers for the kids to classify. The birds are back, too. Ask your students to observe these feathered friends in action. Go for a walk—looking, listening, and smelling spring. Ask the kids to note changes they observe.

THE MEASURES OF MAY
(whole class)
SUPPLIES: celsius indoor/outdoor thermometer
EXPERIENCE: May is a great month for measuring. Have your students check and record the temperature at regular intervals to see how it changes during the day. You might also measure rainfall, windspeed, shadows, and different types of growing things to see how they're changing. If you measured your students in the fall, measure them again. Kids enjoy seeing how they've grown.

AFTER THE STORM
(whole class)
SUPPLIES: a picture of an eroded area
EXPERIENCE: After there's been a heavy spring rain, show your students this picture. Ask them to infer why the erosion was so bad in this location. (Bare soil, loose soil, and a steep slope are all possibilities to consider.) Have the kids work through constructing a hypothesis and designing an experiment that can be done to test their inferences.

USING THE ACTIVITIES:

This month's activities, which appear on pages 149-154, are designed to reinforce what your students have learned about process skills and experiments this year. Before you give the kids each worksheet, review the skills needed to complete it. You might also want to follow up by having the class come up with activities based on the skills used to do the worksheets. Read each activity page in this section before you look at the instructions here.

NOW YOU SEE IT—NOW YOU DON'T, page 149
(center)
SUPPLIES: cotton-tipped swabs or clean paintbrushes, milk, lemon juice, onion juice, white paper, a lamp with a 200-watt bulb (shade removed)
EXPERIENCE: With this activity, you can give your students added practice in three process skills—observing, inferring, and communicating. Before anyone begins, tell the class the story of the secret message sent to John Jay during the American Revolution (see ``Highlights of May'' page 145). Be sure to have the kids share any responses from friends who received the messages.

THAT'S FROG-TASTIC!, pages 150-151
(whole class)
Pass out the quiz first. Use this test to get the kids thinking. Or, ask your students to do research to answer the questions. This activity starts kids classifying frogs by having them identify attributes. Expand on it by asking the children to make a chart and to actually group the frogs listed. You may want the class to find out more about these frogs. Or have students research and classify other types of frogs, such as: the leopard frog, bullfrog, cricket frog, green frog, arum frog, and pickerel frog.

STUCK ON ART, page 152
(whole class)
SUPPLIES: a roll of masking tape, scissors, centimeter rulers
EXPERIENCE: Give each child some tape. As the students work on their designs, have them measure and record the size of each piece of tape after it is placed. When the kids complete their pictures, ask them to look at the pictures carefully and think about how to describe them. Have the students use their observations and the recorded sizes to write the directions. When the children finish, have them test how well they communicated. Ask them to tape a colored construction paper flap over their designs. Next, tell them to exchange directions with someone. Pass out more paper and tape. Have students duplicate the tape design, following the directions they received. When the kids are finished, have them lift the flaps and compare. Take time to allow them to share what was difficult about writing the directions and in what ways these could have been made clearer.

UNDER-COVER OPERATION, page 153*
(whole class)
Challenge your students by having them think through the problem-solving steps of conducting an experiment to test their hypotheses. Encourage the use of critical thinking skills. Write the design of the experiment on the chalkboard as the steps are completed. Have students pool their responses. Then expand this activity by dividing your class into small groups and letting them perform the experiment. Be sure to allow time to discuss the results.

WHAT'S BLOWING?, page 154
(homework)
Here's another chance for kids to practice observing. Use this take-home activity to lead into an exploration of what causes wind and why wind blows harder at some times than it does at others. (Unequal heating causes wind. The warmer air rises and cooler air moves in under it. The greater the difference in temperature, the faster the movement, and the stronger the wind generated.)

*Challenging activity

Now you see it— Now you don't

Here's a chance to use your powers of observation to figure out how invisible ink works.

There are a number of inexpensive, readily available substances that make good invisible ink. Choose one from this list.

milk   lemon juice   onion juice

Use a cotton-tipped swab or a clean paintbrush to write a secret message on a piece of plain white paper with this "ink." Don't make your writing too wet. You don't want the paper to wrinkle, revealing your secret message. Let the letters dry completely.

Hold the paper with the secret message close to a lamp that is lit. Be careful not to let the paper or your fingers get too close to the hot bulb. Watch what happens as the ink warms up.

1. Which ink did you use? _____

2. Describe what happened to the ink as it warmed up.

_____

_____

3. Make an inference about why you think this change took place.

_____

_____

_____

Now, write a letter to a friend using a ballpoint pen and permanent ink. Between the lines of this letter, use invisible ink to write a secret message. But be sure the letter includes step-by-step directions telling your friend how to read the message.

Name _____

That's frog-tastic

Want to find out some amazing facts about frogs? Take this quiz. Read the statements below. Put a T on the blank beside any that you think are true and an F next to any that you believe are false.

1. A frog can weigh as much as a small cat. _____

2. Frogs don't take care of their young. _____

3. Some frogs are poisonous. _____

4. Frogs are always camouflage-colored to help them hide. _____

5. All frogs catch insects with a long, sticky tongue. _____

6. Some frogs can fly. _____

Name _____

150

Quiz answers:

1. True. While most frogs are small, Africa's goliath frog is a giant. It may grow up to a foot long and can weigh more than 10 pounds. However, unlike most frogs, the goliath can't croak.

2. False. In fact, the male Darwin frog of Chile is a super dad. He picks up the eggs with his tongue and deposits them inside his vocal sac. When the young hatch, Daddy opens his mouth and out hop the young frogs.

3. True. Certain types of South American frogs are very poisonous.

4. False. Most frogs are colored for hiding, but South American arrow poison frogs are bright yellow and red. Their color says "leave me alone."

5. False. The African clawed frog doesn't even have a tongue. But since this frog eats underwater, it doesn't need one. It digs insects out of the pond bottom with its clawed hind toes. Then it opens its mouth and sweeps the food inside.

6. False. But don't be surprised to see one go over your head. The Asian gliding frog has extra flaps of skin that let it glide as far as 50 feet from tree top to tree top.

Use what you observed about frogs in this quiz to list at least three attributes that could be used to classify them.

1. _____

2. _____

3. _____

Name _____

Stuck on art

Use strips of masking tape to create a design inside the frame. Write step-by-step directions on the lines below, telling someone who can't see your design how to make an exact copy.

_____

_____

_____

_____

_____

_____

Name _____

Under-cover operation

Answer the questions to design an experiment that could be used to test this hypothesis: The thicker the insulation, the slower the heat is lost.

1. What variable will you need to manipulate?

_____

_____

2. In what way will you change the manipulated variable?

_____

_____

3. What responding variable will you look for?

_____

_____

4. How will you measure the responding variable?

_____

_____

5. What variables will you need to control?

_____

_____

_____

Name _____

What's blowing?

Today, a special instrument called an anemometer is used to measure wind speed. Before the anemometer, the Beaufort scale was the main tool used to tell how strong the wind was blowing. This scale, invented by Sir Francis Beaufort in 1805, related wind speed to what can be seen moving in the wind. The Beaufort scale still provides a useful way to make general observations about the wind's strength.

Read through the Beaufort scale shown below. Every day for a week, look for the signs given in the scale and classify the wind. Record your findings on the chart.

BEAUFORT SCALE

Signs to Watch For:	Type of Wind:
Smoke rises straight up, smoke may drift	Calm
Wind felt on face; leaves rustle	Light breeze
Leaves and small twigs move; flags wave slightly	Gentle breeze
Dust and bits of paper blow about; small branches move; small trees sway; whitecaps on lakes and ponds	Moderate breeze
Large branches move; whole trees sway; difficult to walk against wind	Strong breeze
Trees uprooted, large amount of damage to buldings	Gale
Widespread wind damage	Storm

Wind chart for week starting _____

Day	Time	Type of Wind
Monday		
Tuesday		
Wednesday		
Thursday		
Friday		

Name _____

154

Especially for K-2
Mini-Review

Now that summer is almost here, it is a good idea to review some of the process skills. Classifying and observing have been chosen for this review because these are skills kids are most likely to use on their own. Send your students into summer seeing, hearing, smelling, touching, tasting, *and* categorizing the pleasures of the season.

EXTENDERS:

GROW A GIFT
(center)
SUPPLIES: planting kits for each child, which include: (a plastic-foam cup, a plastic spoon, a sandwich-sized plastic bag) flower seeds, potting soil, plastic wrap, water
EXPERIENCE: To let your students observe a sequence in action, have them grow flowers. Help the kids follow these planting directions:
1. Poke a few drainage holes in the bottom of a plastic-foam cup.
2. Put potting soil in the cup.
3. Plant several seeds in the soil.
4. Open the plastic bag and roll it down to form a saucer.
5. Put the saucer in a warm place that doesn't get too much sun and put the cup on the saucer.
6. Sprinkle two teaspoons (10 milliliters) of water on the soil.
7. Cover the cup with a piece of the plastic wrap.

Have the children water the seeds every other day by pouring water into the saucer. Remove the plastic wrap when the seeds sprout. Remind the kids to water their plants and to observe the growth changes. (The plants may be taken home as Mother's Day gifts!)

FEET FIRST
(whole class)
Go for a walk outdoors on a sunny day and give your students a chance to use their feet as personal measuring units. Have them measure the distance between trees or other landmarks, the distance around a sandbox, or a flagpole's shadow. Do students get different measurements? Discuss why this is so.

EYE BET YOU CAN
(whole class)
Give your students one more challenge for their observational skills. Ask the kids to point out things in a particular color. Start with green, then focus on brown, red, yellow blue, and other colors.

USING THE ACTIVITIES:

The activities that review classifying and observing appear on pages 157-160. Be sure to go over the skills your students use to complete each worksheet. You might also want to provide follow-up activities that give kids practice in other process skills. An individual page reference for each worksheet is included below. Read through the activity before you look at the teacher notes.

ONE MORE, page 157
(whole class)
Here's another chance for your students to practice classifying. Help the kids think through what attribute each set has in common. Then have them decide which of the possible extra items has that same attribute.

WRONG SEASON, page 158
(whole class)
Help your students become good observers and use memories of seasonal things with this activity. Introduce the activity with a class discussion of what kids expect to see and do in the summer and in the winter. If winter and summer are much the same where you live, display pictures of winter in the northern United States. After the children complete the activity, let them color the pictures.

GO ON A FINGER HUNT, page 159
(whole class)
In this activity, your students have an opportunity to focus on observing, using their sense of touch. Display the samples on a bulletin board. After your students have had an opportunity to observe all the samples, call on them to describe something fuzzy, soft, scratchy, and slick, using their touch, vision, and even hearing.

WHEN I GROW UP, page 160
(whole class)
This is a fun activity which encourages kids to make a prediction about themselves. You may want to extend this by having your students bring in pictures of themselves as babies. Then ask them to describe ways in which they've already changed. These should include being able to do more, as well as simply growing bigger.

One more

How are the things in each of these sets alike? Draw a line from each set to one more thing that could belong to it.

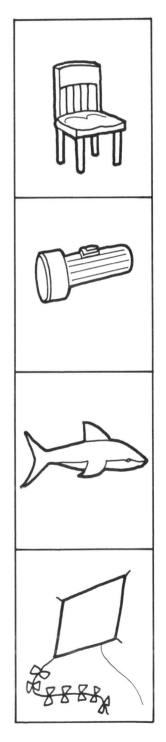

1.

2.

3.

4.

Wrong season

Can you spot what does not belong in this picture? Put an X on each thing you would expect to see during a different season.

Name _____

Go on a finger hunt

The words above each box describe the way things feel. Find something that fits each of those descriptions. Then cut out a small piece and glue or tape it in the box. Be sure to ask it it's okay before you cut your sample.

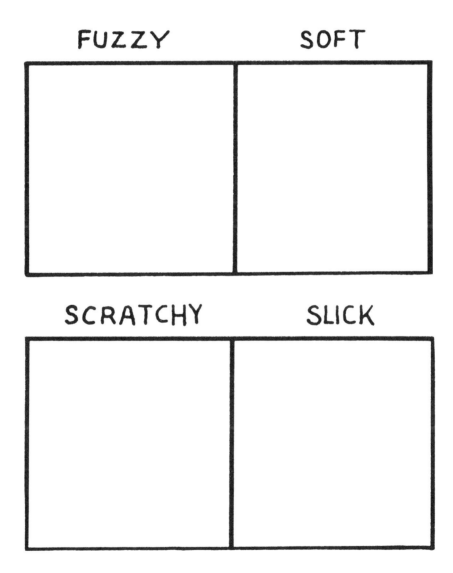

FUZZY   SOFT

SCRATCHY   SLICK

Name _____

When I grow up

Look at childhood pictures of your mom, dad, or an adult. What are two ways this person has changed?

Draw a picture of what you think you'll look like as an adult.

What is something you think you'll like about being grown up?

_____

What is something you'll miss about being a child?

_____

Name _____

Super summer send-homes

The activities contained in this chapter are designed for students to take home and work on independently. These activities are fun-packed opportunities for kids to continue building upon the basic science process skill in problem-solving situations. You might also notify parents of the activities and ask them to assist students with completing these activities.

There is something in this set for all ages. Choose the send-home that best fits your students' grade level.

Have a happy summer.

Go exploring

Hot on the trail

Do you want to track some wild game? Put a little pile of granulated sugar on the ground. How long does it take before some ants find your bait? Watch the ants at work. What do they do with the sugar? Do the ants come from all directions or do they come and go along a definite route? See if you can follow the ants back to their home. You may want to make a trip to the library to find out more about the interesting life of ants.

Treasure hunt

Hide something for a friend, then make a map that will guide your friend to the treasure. Use compass headings for directions or right and left turns—plus the number of steps needed. Can you draw a map that will communicate your directions clearly? Have your friend hide a treasure and make a map for you, too. Who can find the treasure first?

162

Tracking down tracks

How many copies of animal tracks can you collect? You'll need a storage-size self-sealing plastic bag, several sandwich-size plastic bags, plaster of Paris powder, 15 to 30 milliliters (one to two tablespoons) of salt, a canteen, water, a plastic shopping bag, a scissors and different sizes of plastic soft-drink bottles. First, prepare your track pack. Pour the plaster powder into the large plastic bag and mix in the salt. Seal this bag carefully so the powder won't spill out. Now fill the canteen with water. Next, squeeze one of the plastic bottles flat and cut across the bottle, making a ring 10 centimeters (4 inches) high. Cut a ring from each of the other bottles in the same way. Put these track-pack items and the small plastic bags in the shopping bag. Then go hunting for animal tracks. You'll find them where the ground is bare and not too sandy. The best time to look is after a rain when the soil is drying out. When you spot a track, pick it clean of any leaves or twigs. Next, surround the track with a plastic ring and push the ring down into the ground a little. Then, prepare the plaster. First, transfer some plaster powder to a small bag (use enough powder to cover the track with a coating about three inches thick) and then add some water. Zip the bag and gently massage it until the water and powder are mixed. The plaster should be about the thickness of pancake batter. Now partially open the bag and squeeze it as you pour the plaster into the track and fill the ring up to about a half inch from the top. Once the track cast is hard, carefully pull it up, holding on to the top of the ring. Put the cast in a plastic bag to protect it while you collect others. Let it set overnight before you brush it clean.

How many different attributes can you identify that you could use to group the tracks you collect? Arrange the casts in a display. Ask your local librarian where to look for books that can help you identify animal tracks.

Start a sunflower farm

Don't worry, you don't need much land! A little plot or even a big pot will do. Dig up the soil so it's soft and crumbly. Buy a packet of seeds and plant them following the package directions.

How big is big?

Think of a least three different ways to measure your sunflowers once they start to grow, such as height, number of leaves, diameter of the flower head, and so forth. Then measure your sunflowers daily in each category and make a chart to show each plant's growth. You may want to raise several different varieties to see which is the sunflower world champion.

Just like clockwork

Sunflowers are said to turn their heads to follow the sun's path across the sky. Is this fact or fiction? Observe your sunflowers to find out. Ask your local librarian to help you find information about sunflower growth.

Pretty seedy

How many seeds are in one giant sunflower? To find out, you'll need a large paper bag and a kitchen scale. After the flower has dried, break it apart and pick out the seeds, putting them in the bag. Then weigh the bag. Next weigh one ounce of seeds. Count how many seeds were in that one-ounce sample. Weigh and count two more one-ounce samples. Then figure out the average number of seeds in a one-ounce sample by adding up the three totals and dividing by 3. Weigh all of the seeds together and multiply the number of ounces by the average number of seeds per ounce to predict how many seeds are in the sunflower.

Make a splash

When it's hot, being all wet can feel pretty good. So as the summer heats up, dive into these investigations.

Ever notice how much cooler you feel when you climb out of the pool dripping wet? But does being wet really make you cooler? To find out, you'll need two indoor/outdoor thermometers and two identical squares of cotton cloth. Place the two thermometers side by side in a sunny spot. Wait 15 minutes. Then check and record the temperature of each thermometer. Next, wet one of the cloths and lay it over the bulb end of one thermometer. Cover the bulb end of the other thermometer with the dry cloth. Wait another 15 minutes. Then check and record the temperatures. Which thermometer showed the biggest drop in temperature?

166

Drips and drops

SUPPLIES: To do these tests on water drops, you'll need yellow, red, and blue food coloring, three glasses of water, a sheet of waxed paper, a toothpick, and soap.

Line up the glasses of water on a flat surface. Then put a few drops of yellow food coloring in the first glass of water. Add red food coloring to a second glass and blue to a third glass. Now sprinkle drops of each on a sheet of the waxed paper. Observe the shape of these drops. Try pushing the colored drops into each other with the toothpick. What happens to the size of the drops? The shape? The color? Now try pulling the drops apart—making several smaller drops out of one big one. Is it easy or hard to do? What would happen if you added a tiny bit of soap to the water? Try it and make fresh drops. Does the soapy water react any differently?

Dig in

You can go to the beach or the sandbox for these explorations.

This old castle

Give step-by-step directions for building a sand castle. You may want to build one yourself and write down the steps to follow as you work. Try to include helpful hints. For example, you might say that wet sand is better than dry for castle construction.

Nitty gritty

Use a magnifying glass to take a close look at sand. What colors do you see? Are there pieces of different kinds of rock? Can you see bits of sea shell? Describe the sizes and shapes of these tiny particles. Are the grains rounded or do they have sharp points? Rub some between your fingers and tell how it feels. Does the sand feel different wet than dry?

Sand leaks

That's right. Water runs right through sand. But suppose you wanted to perform an experiment to test this hypothesis: As the grain size increases, the rate of water draining through the sand increases. What will be your manipulating variable? In what way will you change the manipulating variable? What will be your responding variable? How will you measure the responding variable? What variables will you need to control? Perform the experiment you design to find out what happens.

Zoo safari

Summer is the perfect time to go to the zoo. Here are some activities to help you enjoy your visit even more.

Zoo awards

Keep track of the different animals you see at the zoo. Which animal is the biggest? The smallest? The fattest? Which animal has the longest neck? The biggest horns? The longest tail? The biggest ears? Can you think of any other special records to award the animals you observe?

What's for dinner

Animals are usually divided into three groups by what they choose to eat: herbivores (plant eaters), carnivores (meat eaters), and omnivores (eat both). Find at least two animals at the zoo that fit into each category at mealtime. Check the signs posted near displays for this information. Or try to be present at mealtime to observe what's being served. Are the diets of any animals limited to only one particular kind of plant or food?

170

Herd it through the grapevine

Some animals like to live in groups. Others prefer to live alone. Which zoo animals obviously prefer to live in groups? Which is the largest group of animals at the zoo? For more information about the animals, read the signs near the displays.

Got you covered!

Can you spot at least one animal that has each of these coverings: 1. Bare or nearly bare skin; 2. Fur; 3. Feathers; 4. Scales. Take a close look at the fur of polar bears. You may be surprised to learn that, while the fur appears white, the individual hairs are actually transparent and hollow. And beneath its fur, the polar bear's skin is black. This special coloring and hollow fur acts like a solar collector, trapping light energy which produces heat that is absorbed by the bear's skin. The polar bear's covering is just right for the cold arctic area where it normally lives. Find at least two other animals that are also dressed for living in a particular climate.

Beautiful babies

Do any of the animals have babies? Perhaps the zoo you're visiting has a special nursery section you can view. Check out these points when observing animal babies.
1. Other than being smaller, do the youngsters look similar to the adults? If not, in what ways are the babies different?
2. Is the baby on its own? Is at least one parent providing care? Can you tell which parent is taking care of the baby? In what way is that parent providing care?

Answer key

14 Sun Prints Don't Last—2) It becomes lighter. 3) Dark images of things printed seem to wash out. 4) The paper becomes darker, images of things printed remain light.

16 Eye Fooled You—3) When pages are flipped slowly, the image may not appear to move at all. The faster the pages are flipped, the smoother the movement becomes.

17 It's A Matter of Tilt—The pennies shine and have a small circle of bright light around them and a small shadow; the pennies appear less bright, the circle of light will be more spread out but less bright, and the shadow will be much longer.

18 As the Leaf Turns—Answers will vary, but the colored leaf will probably be drier and less flexible so it may be more "crackly". It may smell different and the surface may feel less waxy. It feels corky.

19 Butter Up—1) Touch, taste, smell, sight. Answers will vary, but the students may state that the cream has a sweet or buttery smell, feels greasy and thick, tastes sweet. 2) It becomes thick and fluffy. 3) Answers will vary, but the students may state that the butter looks yellowish white, is thick, feels cool, is solid, tastes sweet, and has no noticeable smell. 4) It has become more solid. There is a slight color change. Other answers are possible. 5) Answers will vary.

20 Moo Mystery—1) One leaves a greasy film. 2) Yes, B is thicker. Descriptions will vary. 3) Both feel wet. A feels more watery and B feels thicker, slicker, and greasier. 4) A is milk and B is whipping cream. It's thicker and greasier.

21 Good to the Core—1) Answers will vary, but should include: differences in size, shape, skin color, skin thickness, flesh color, and texture. 2) Answers will vary. 3) Answers will vary, but the students should be able to describe some flavor and texture differences. 4) An-

swers will vary, but could include weighing the whole apple or letting a slice of each dry and comparing which is then most appealing.

34-35 Crater Capers—1) Something hard that falls from space and strikes the surface. 2) Answers will vary, but should describe a hole. 3) The hole is deeper. 4) Material splattering out of the hole, crumbled material from the meteorite.

36-37 3-2-1 Blastoff— 1) Answers will vary. 2) One possible solution is to blow it up more.

40-41 In the Can—1) So Fine & Chef's Choice. 2) So Fine & Yummy Soup. 3) So Fine. 4) Answers will vary, but two possibilities are calories and expiration dates longer than a year.

42 Unbe-leaf-able—Answers will vary, but could include presence of holes, size and leaflets.

55-56 A Lot of Hot Air—1) Answers will vary. It looked the same as at the beginning of the experiment. 2) Answers will vary. It was still the same. 3) At least three times. 4) The flame heats air in the balloon. As the air gets hotter, it expands, inflating the balloon.

57-58 The Great Paper Airplane Race—It lets you see that any difference in the way the two airplanes fly is the result of the design change you made. 1) Location of launch site, position of your arm and amount of force used to launch the airplanes, and wind strength and wind direction. 2) Position of your arm and amount of force used to launch the airplanes. 3) Answers will vary.

59-60 Hamburger Test—Amount of fat in meat, size and shape of patties. Answers will vary. There is no right or wrong answer as long as good scientific method was used. Because the results from a test that is made just once can be a freak occurrence. If the same or very similar results are obtained during three or more tests, these results

172

can be expected to be what will usually occur. 1) Ketchup 2) Onion 3) Cheese 4) Mustard 5) Pickle

62 Gotta Have Heart—1) Heart rate while still. 2) That allowed every test to start with the heart rate normal. 3) Exercising speed is a variable that needs to be controlled. Exercising faster can change the results. 4) Makes it beat faster—the more strenuous the exercise, the faster the heart beats.

63 Cold Challenge—1) Answers will vary. 2) Answers will vary, but should include ice cube size and all conditions should be the same for the test and the control except one. 3) Answers will vary. 4) Answers will vary, but should clearly take into account the experiment's results.

73-74 Make Your Own Music—1) High pitched. 2) Got lower. 3) Being stretched more makes the sound deeper. 4) Stretch the rubber band longer and longer while plucking it and listen to what happens to the sound. 5) The sound does get lower and lower as the band is stretched more and more. 6) It also produced an increasingly deeper sound. 7) Lower. 8) An even thicker one. Because the thicker the rubber band, the deeper the pitch of the sound it produces.

75-76 Ring Reading—1) 8 years old. 2) There was 1 year when it was really dry and 1 year with extra rain. 3) 15 years. 4) There were 3 years of drought, 2 years with extra rain and 1 year when either a fire or lightning hit the tree. 5) Check a lot of other trees in the area because while they would all be affected by drought, they probably wouldn't all be attacked by insects.

77-78 Holiday Lights—The bulb lights. Brass will not complete the circuit.

79 Light Puzzles

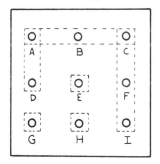 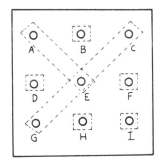

80 What's for Dinner—Test them by observing each of these birds. Or check books about these birds.

91 Words You Can Feel—Drums.

92-93 Talking Wire—Answers will vary, but should express ideas clearly and in a logical sequence.

96 Pie? Oh My!—Order should be 7, 1, 9, 6, 5, 4, 2, 3, 8.

100-101 Funny Puppy—1) Puppy ran after his ball. 2) Billy helped Puppy get his ball. 3) Puppy got all muddy. 4) Then Billy gave Puppy a bath.

102 Learn to Use the Telephone—1) Answers will vary. 2) Dial tone. 3) Hang up and try again later. 4) Deposit a quarter or whatever amount is required in the area where the call is made. Dial tone. Will come back. 5) 0-Zero. 6) Answers will vary, depending on what parents or guardians prefer.

107-108 On Fire—1) Eight pints. 2) Answers will depend on how long the candle burned in 1 pint and 2 pints of air, but the prediction should be proportionally greater than those amounts of time. 3) Answers will vary, but should indicate a point between the times for the pint and quart. 4) The second one. Because this prediction is within a pattern. The first prediction goes beyond the pattern. Other variables might affect burning times.

109 Sun Watchers—1) Answers will vary. 2) Should feel very confident because pattern is projected just one day farther. 3) Answers will vary. 4) No, because the prediction goes so far beyond the known pattern. You don't know if the pattern will continue or change.

110-111 Crystal Clear—The granite; The granite; Because the pattern suggests that the fastest-cooling molten rock should have the fewest and smallest crystals, and there are no crystals visible in the samples. Answers will vary, but should include changes in crystal size, shape and color. Find a way to make crystals form more slowly such as keeping them in a cool place.

112 Phone Book—1) Answers will vary. 2) Answers will vary. 3) Answers will vary.

122-123 Tree-mendous—1) Usually no. 2) Answers will vary, but should include amount of sunlight the branch receives and number of leaves it has, whether any other branch is in its way. Mystery Trees—Maple; Redwood; Sycamore; Elm; Pine; Oak; Willow; Birch; Ash; Palm; Cedar; Walnut

127 How Cold Is It—1) Answers will vary. 2) Answers will vary. 3) Check the temperature in full sun at a windy place and at a place sheltered from the wind.

137 Ice Test—1) Object: size, shape, thickness, frozenness, and presence of holes. Environmental: air temperature, amount of sunlight, wind, direction, strength of wind, insulation thickness, efficiency of insulation, humidity, and amount of friction. 2) Answers will vary, but could be any of the above listed. 3) Melting rate. 4) Answers will vary, but could include weight of ice before and after the test, or collect melted liquid after the test.

138 Just Leafy—Answers will vary, but could include: 1) As the number of hours of direct sunlight increases, the leaf-opening rate also increases. 2) As the amount of water available increases, the leaf-opening rate also increases. 3) As the height of the plant increases, the leaf-opening rate decreases. All answers should predict a relationship between the manipulating and responding variables.

139 Stretching It—1) Temperature. 2) It was increased at 10°F intervals. 3) The amount of stretch in the rubber band. 4)

By finding out the length of each rubber band.

140 Big Blow—1) Wind Speed. 2) Answers will vary, but could include changing how often the water is fanned in a minute—for example, ten, twenty and thirty times. 3) Answers will vary, but could include weighing the water remaining after the test or measuring the depth of this water. 4) Lists will vary, but should include: size and shape of container, the amount of water, water temperature, air temperature, humidity, exposure to sunlight, type of object used to fan the water, and force used in fanning.

149 Now You See It—1) Answers will vary. 2) Ink became dark. 3) Answers will vary, but could include that the heat caused a chemical change.

150-151 Frog-Tastic—Attributes: size, color, type of care given young, poisonous, have a tongue, ability to glide.

153 Under Cover—1) The thickness of insulating material. 2) Answers will vary, but should list a set of steps for increasing the thickness of the insulating material such as by 2.5 centimeters (1 inch), 5 centimeters (2 inches), and 7.5 centimeters (3 inches). 3) Heat loss. 4) Check the temperature reading on a thermometer. 5) Answers will vary, but could include size of the insulating material, type of insulating material, type of thermometer, way the insulation is wrapped around the thermometer, air temperature, exposure to sunlight, air movement and humidity.

Using the task cards

Pages 177-191 include six sets of reproducible task cards. Each set focuses on a particular process skill—observing, classifying, communicating, inferring, predicting, or measuring. These cards are designed to reinforce what your students have learned about the featured skill and to provide added practice. The individual page references in this section will help you find the cards so you can read through them before you look at the supply lists, instructions, and answer keys found here.

BROKEN RAINBOW, page 177
SUPPLIES: poster board, one piece each of red, blue, and yellow cellophane, scissors, masking tape.
EXPERIENCE: On a piece of the poster board, draw the paddle shape shown. Cut the shape out and use it as a pattern to make five more shapes. Then tape the piece of red cellophane to one of the paddle shapes, covering the hole and trimming. Next, put another paddle shape on top of the first one and tape the edges together. Make the blue and yellow paddles in the same way.
ANSWERS: 1-3: Answers will vary. 4: Yellow plus red becomes orange; yellow plus blue becomes green; red plus blue becomes purple.

SECRET COLORS, page 177
SUPPLIES: yellow, red, and blue food coloring, a small paper cup, a tall water glass, water, scissors, a cotton-tipped swab, enough coffee filters to have one for each child.
EXPERIENCE: Pour equal amounts of each food coloring into the paper cup and mix.
ANSWERS: 1: It moves up through the filter paper. 2: It is dark muddy brown. 3: It is carried with the water. As it moves, the colors separate and spread out. 4: A rainbow of red, yellow, and blue.

HARVEST TIME, page 179
SUPPLIES: squash seeds, popcorn kernels, sunflower seeds, navy beans, kidney beans, sesame seeds.
ANSWERS: List of attributes will vary, but could include sizes, colors, and shapes. Chart classifications will vary. The nuts are sorted by texture.

JUST ADD WATER, page 181
SUPPLIES: salt, baking soda, sugar, sand, plaster of Paris, water, a measuring cup, a teaspoon, Popsicle sticks, enough clear plastic cups to have five for each child.
ANSWERS: Chart: Dissolves—salt, sugar, baking soda. Does not dissolve—sand, plaster of Paris. 1: Answers will vary, but could include gritty, soft, sticky. 2: All the powders are the same color. 3: Used in foods—salt, sugar, baking soda. Not used in foods—sand, plaster of Paris.

WHO YOU GONNA CALL? page 183
SUPPLIES: encyclopedias, books on inventors.
EXPERIENCE: Encourage students to be creative when they write their questions. Have kids share their choices of favorite inventor with the class and discuss why they made their decisions.

PERSON TO PERSON, page 183
SUPPLIES: two empty metal cans (soup cans work well), a hammer, a nail, a button, a cardboard tube, 6 meters (20 feet) of monofilament fishing line.
EXPERIENCE: Use the hammer and nail to punch a small hole in the bottom of each can. Thread one end of the line through the hole in one of the cans and tie this end to a button as shown in the diagram. Then thread the other end of the line through the hole in the second can and tape that end to the cardboard tube as shown. Wrap the line around this "reel."
ANSWERS: 1: It conducts well enough to remain clear up to 4½ (15 feet). At a greater distance, it is more difficult to hear. 2: The vibrations will not conduct well through the limp line. 3: Answers will vary but could include that the sound is less clear or can't be heard at all.

THAT SINKING FEELING, page 185
SUPPLIES: one paper cup for each child, a quart jar, a long-handled spoon, water, gravel, sand, clay.
EXPERIENCE: To save materials and time in cleaning up, you could make the initial mixture and pour it in the jar yourself. Then kids can stir and observe the mixture and infer why it settled the way it did.
ANSWERS: 1: Answers will vary, but could

include bigger and heavier particles settle more quickly. 2: By repeating the settling test with a mixture of large lightweight plastic-foam pieces, sand, and clay.

THE MYSTERY BOX, page 185
SUPPLIES: a shoe box, scissors, an old tube sock, duct tape, two unwrapped hard peppermint candies.
EXPERIENCE: In one side of the box, cut a slot that is just big enough for a child's hand to slide through. Then cut the toe off the sock and tape this pocket to the inside of the box, with the mouth of the pocket spread out around the slot. Now, place the candy in the box, put on the lid, and tape the box shut.
ANSWERS: Answers will vary but the observations should be based on the information each sense provides and the inferences should be directly related to these observations .

BE A SWINGER, page 187
SUPPLIES: a piece of string 40 centimeters (16 inches) long, a metal nut, a yardstick, books, masking tape.
EXPERIENCE: To set up the pendulum, tie the nut to one end of the string. Then place the yardstick so that it projects out over the side of a table, using a stack of books to anchor it in place. Now tape the free end of the string to the projecting end of the stick, making the pendulum exactly 30 centimeters (1 foot) long from its anchor point to its bob (the nut).
ANSWERS: 1: It will take less time. 2: Very confident, because it follows the pattern observed in the investigation. 3: Less confident, because it's too far removed from the pattern.

THAT'S ATTRACTIVE, page 189
SUPPLIES: a D cell battery, a 1-meter (40-inch) piece of copper wire, a steel nail, a battery holder (available at hobby stores that sell electronic equipment).
EXPERIENCE: To build an electromagnet, strip about 2½ centimeters (1 inch) from each end of the wire piece. Also be sure the free end of each battery holder wire is stripped. Now attach one end of the wire piece to the end of one of the battery holder wires, twisting the bare wires together to join them securely. Then wrap the wire piece around the nail five times (see diagram), leaving about a 60 centimerter (24-inch) tail. Insert the battery in the holder. To turn the magnet on, twist together the end of this tail and the end of the battery holder wire.
ANSWERS: 1: Answers will vary but, the number should fit the pattern shown by the student's chart. 2: Very confident, because it is within the observed pattern. 3: No, because this prediction is too far beyond the observed pattern.

BIG FOOT, page 191
EXPERIENCE: This task card is a really tough challenge for kids with great math skills. Before students work on the activity, be sure to go over how to convert the heights or distances into centimeters. Then explain to the children that after they convert each measurement, they must divide it by 33.75. Also point out that only whole sneakers need be counted. You'll need these measurements: the height of World Trade Center Tower Two, 409 meters (1362 feet); maximum length of a regulation-size basketball court, 29 meters (94 feet); the distance from New York City to Los Angeles, 4477 kilometers (2776 miles); the height of Mount Everest, 8,848 meters (29,028 feet).
ANSWERS: 1: 1,212. 2: 85. 3: 132,266,666. 4: 26,216. 5: Answers will vary.

EVERY STEP COUNTS, page 191
SUPPLIES: string, chalk, or tape.
EXPERIENCE: You'll need to set up a course kids can walk to measure the double-step. On a big open area, such as a parking lot or open field, mark a starting line. Then place another marker 70 meters (233 feet) away.
ANSWERS: Answers will vary depending on the actual distance to each of these places and the length of each child's double-step.

176

Task cards

BROKEN RAINBOW

Observing

What if you could break a rainbow and collect each of its beautiful colors to look through anytime you want? Pretend that the special paddles your teacher prepared for you are made with pieces of a rainbow. Use the paddles to answer these questions:

1. Take an object and look through the red paddle and then the blue one. Other than its color, does anything else appear different?
2. Look at another object through the yellow paddle and then through the blue paddle. With which paddle is it easier to tell whether the object's surface is smooth or rough?
3. Look at something in the distance through each of the paddles. Which color makes it easiest to see details?
4. Now try overlapping the different paddles. Look through yellow plus red, yellow plus blue, and red plus blue. Describe how this changes the colors you see in each case.

SECRET COLORS

Observing

Your teacher has used food coloring to prepare a secret mixture. To find out what colors are in the mixture, follow the directions below. Then answer the questions as you watch what happens.

First, take a coffee filter and cut it as shown in diagram 1. Then, fold down the narrow piece of the filter to form a wick. Next, pour a small amount of water into a glass. Place the filter on top of the glass as shown in diagram 2. (The bottom of the wick should just touch the water.) Now, use a cotton-tipped swab to dab a small amount of the secret mixture above the water line on the wick.

1. What does the water do when the bottom of the wick touches it?
2. Describe the color of the secret mixture when it first touches the filter.
3. What happens to the secret mixture when the water reaches it?
4. What do you see as the color mixture spreads out?

Task cards

Classifying

HARVEST TIME

Carefully examine the seeds. Then list at least three attributes that could be used to sort these seeds. Prepare a chart like the one below to show how you would classify these seeds.

Attribute	Have It	Don't Have It

These nuts have already been sorted. Which attribute was used to classify them? ☐ Size   ☐ Texture   ☐ Color

Common Measures
3 teaspoons = 1 Tablespoon
Cup = 8 ounces or
    16 Tablespoons
Pint = 16 ounces or 2 cups
Quart = 32 ounces or 2 pints
US gallon = 64 ounces or 4 quarts
12 inches = 1 foot
3 feet = 1 yard
Mile = 5280 feet or 1760 yards

Metric Measures
10 milligrams = 1 gram
1000 grams = 1 kilogram
1000 milliliters = 1 liter
10 millimeters = 1 centimeter
100 centimeters = 1 meter
1000 meters = 1 kilometer

Metric Equivalents
(approximate)
Ounce = 28.35 grams
Gram = .035 ounces
Inch = 25.4 millimeters
Millimeter = .038 inches
1 foot = .0305 meter
1 yard = .91 meters
1 meter = 3.28 feet or 39.4 inches

Temperature
Celsius: 0° water freezes
    100° water boils
Fahrenheit: 32° water freezes
    212° water boils
Celsius = $\frac{5}{9}$(F°-32)
Fahrenheit = ($\frac{9}{5}$C°)+32

Metric Conversions
(approximate)
ounces × 28.35 = grams
grams × .035 = ounces

pounds × .45 = kilograms
kilograms × 2.2 = pounds

quarts × .95 = liters
liters × 1.05 = quarts

US gallons × 3.8 = liters
liters × .264 = gallons

inches × 25.4 = millimeters
millimeters × .038 = inches

inches × 2.54 = centimeters
centimeters × .038 = inches

feet × .305 = meters
meters × 3.3 = feet

yards × .91 = meters
meters × 1.1 = yards

Distance
miles × 1.61 = kilometers
kilometers × .62 = miles

Task cards

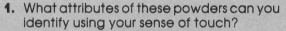

JUST ADD WATER 1

Classifying

Your teacher has provided samples of five powders: salt, baking soda, sugar, sand, and plaster of Paris. Line up five clear plastic cups. Then pour one-fourth cup water into each. Next test the powders, one at a time, to see if they will dissolve in water: Add one teaspoon of the powder to the water in one of the cups, then stir with a popsicle stick and watch closely. Does the powder actually dissolve? Or does it only settle to the bottom? Test the other powders in the same way. Now copy the chart and complete it. Then answer the questions.

1. What attributes of these powders can you identify using your sense of touch?

2. Why would color not be a good attribute to use in sorting the powders?

3. Since you know what the powders are, sort them into these two groups—those that are used in foods and those that aren't

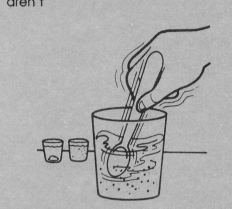

JUST ADD WATER 2

Classifying

Powder	Dissolves	Does not dissolve

Task cards

WHO YOU GONNA CALL?

Pretend that through magic you can make a telephone call to each of the inventors listed below. Write one question that you would like to ask each of them. You may want to find out something about each inventor's life and work before you decide on your question.

1. Ben Franklin
2. Louis Braille
3. Samuel F. B. Morse
4. Robert Goddard

5. Thomas A. Edison
6. Orville Wright
7. Alexander Graham Bell
8. Chester Greenwood

If you could call one inventor, which would you most like to talk to? Why?

PERSON TO PERSON

Your teacher has prepared a pair of tin-can telephones for you and a partner to test out. Here's what to do. Find someone to work with.

1. Move the telephones 1½ meters (5 feet) apart and try talking to your partner. Try again, changing the distance between the telephones to 3 meters (10 feet) and then to 4½ meters (15 feet). Be sure the line is stretched tight each time. Can you hear just as well at each of these distances or does the sound become less clear the farther the telephones are apart? How clear is the sound if you stretch the line all the way out?

2. Let the line go limp. Does this effect how well sound travels along the line?

3. Stretch the line around a corner. How well can you hear now?

Task cards

THAT SINKING FEELING

In a paper cup, mix together two tablespoons of each of these materials: gravel, sand, and clay. Pour this mixture into a quart jar that is half full of water. Stir well. Then let the muddy solution sit for several hours or until the particles settle and the water is nearly clear.

Look closely. You'll be able to see three layers: gravel on the bottom, sand in the middle, and clay grains on top.

1. Write two inferences that explain why the gravel settled to the bottom before the sand or clay.
2. How can you test the inference that bigger particles settle first?

THE MYSTERY BOX

Your teacher has hidden something in the box. Follow the steps below, making observations and inferences to figure out what the mystery object is.

1. Shake the box and listen. List at least three observations about what you hear. What do you infer must be in the box, based on what you observed?
2. Next, sniff the box. Describe what you observed. Do you still think that your original inference is correct? If not, tell what your new inference is.
3. Finally, reach through the flap and feel. Describe what you observed this time. Do you want to keep or change your inference now?

Task cards

BE A SWINGER 1

Predicting

Your teacher has set up a pendulum for you. The pendulum is 30 centimeters (1 foot) long at its full length. Hold onto the pendulum bob (the metal nut), pull it back and release it. Use a clock with a second hand to time how many seconds it takes the pendulum to complete one arc—one swing forward and back. Record this number on the chart. Do this test twice more and record the results. Then average all the recorded times by adding them up and dividing by 3—the number of tests you made. Next, shorten the string to each of the other two lengths shown on the chart, repeat the tests, and record and average the results.

1. Predict whether you think a pendulum 10 centimeters long will take more or less time to complete one arc than one 30 centimeters long.
2. How confident do you feel about this prediction? Why?
3. Would you feel more or less confident making a prediction about a pendulum 100 centimeters long? Why?

BE A SWINGER 2

Predicting

Length of Pendulum	Time it takes to complete one arc			
	1	2	3	Average
30 centimeters				
20 centimeters				
15 centimeters				

Task cards

THAT'S ATTRACTIVE 1

Predicting

Use the electromagnet your teacher prepared. Start with five coils around the nail and test how many paper clips the magnet can pick up. Record this quantity on the chart. Do this test two more times and record the results. Then average all the quantities by adding them up and dividing by 3—the number of tests you made. Next, increase the number of coils as shown on the chart, repeat the tests, and record and average the results.

1. Predict how many clips the electromagnet will be able to attract with 25 coils.

2. How confident do you feel about this prediction? Why?

3. Would you feel confident predicting how many clips the electromagnet could attract with 200 coils? Why?

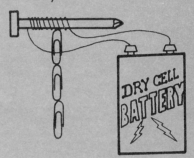

THAT'S ATTRACTIVE 2

Predicting

Coils	Test 1	Test 2	Test 3	Average
5				
10				
15				
20				

Task cards

BIG FOOT

Measuring

That's a nickname you can give Kareem Abdul-Jabbar, star of the Los Angeles Laker's basketball team. The size 17 sneakers he wears are 33.75 centimeters (13 1/2 inches) long. Pretend that you can use one of Kareem's giant sneakers for measuring. How many size 17 sneakers, lined up toe to heel, would it take to measure each of these?
1. The height of a regulation-size basketball court
2. The height of the World Trade Center's Tower Two, in New York
3. The distance from New York City to Los Angeles
4. The height of Mount Everest
5. Your height

EVERY STEP COUNTS

Measuring

One way to measure long distances easily is the double-step. A double-step is the distance covered in one step, counting only steps by the same foot (right or left). To measure using the double-step, you first need to find out the average distance you cover in one double-step.

Your teacher has set up a test course. Decide whether to keep track of your right or left steps. Then walk from the starting line to the end marker and back. Take normal steps and count each time your chosen foot hits the ground.

Next, divide 40 meters (131 feet), the total distance you covered, by the number of double steps you took. The answer will tell you how many meters you cover in one double-step.

Now, measure distances by counting double-steps and multiplying that number by the meters you cover in a double-step. Use your double-steps to find out how far it is from your classroom door to each of these places:

1. The librarian's desk
2. The door to the principal's office
3. The school's front door
4. The cafeteria

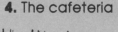